LAST

DON

STANDING

LAST
DON
STANDING

THE SECRET LIFE OF MOB BOSS
RALPH NATALE

DAN PEARSON

AND

LARRY McSHANE

Thomas Dunne Books
St. Martin's Press
New York

THOMAS DUNNE BOOKS.
An imprint of St. Martin's Press.

LAST DON STANDING. Copyright © 2017 by Dan Pearson and
Larry McShane. All rights reserved. Printed in the United States of
America. For information, address St. Martin's Press, 175 Fifth Avenue,
New York, N.Y. 10010.

www.thomasdunnebooks.com
www.stmartins.com

Photos courtesy of Ralph Natale and Dan Pearson.

Designed by Omar Chapa

The Library of Congress Cataloging-in-Publication Data is available
upon request.

ISBN 978-1-250-09587-9 (hardcover)
ISBN 978-1-250-09588-6 (e-book)

Our books may be purchased in bulk for promotional, educational, or
business use. Please contact your local bookseller or the Macmillan
Corporate and Premium Sales Department at 1-800-221-7945, extension
5442, or by e-mail at MacmillanSpecialMarkets@macmillan.com.

First Edition: March 2017

10 9 8 7 6 5 4 3 2 1

For the McShane family: Margie, Megan, Joseph, and Stacey.

*For Dan, the 11-year-old homeless boy, alone and
sleeping inside an abandoned car in East New York.
Dreams do come true.*

CONTENTS

Acknowledgments...ix
Cast of Characters.......................................xi
Prologue: Christmas Day 1973.............................1

1. A Sit-Down with the Boss..............................5
2. Kids in Philly..11
3. Love and Devotion.....................................18
4. New York, New York....................................28
5. The Rise of the Docile Don............................32
6. Mob Heavyweights......................................42
7. Doing the Work..48
8. Where the Sand Is Turnin' to Gold.....................51
9. An Irish Wake...65
10. The Razor's Edge.....................................68
11. Union Sundown..80
12. Roll of the Dice.....................................86
13. Meeting Mr. Stanfa...................................91
14. Something's Burning..................................94
15. Angelo Bruno, What Has Happened to You?..............103

16. Et Tu, Tony Bananas? — 110
17. The Wake — 120
18. Rise of the Chicken Man — 133
19. They Blew Up the Chicken Man — 141
20, Life in Lewisburg — 155
21. Mr. Natale Goes to Washington — 159
22. A Mafia Prince — 167
23. Stanfa Redux — 178
24. A Marriage of Mob-Style Convenience — 183
25. Don't Call It a Comeback — 206
26. Where Did It All Go Wrong? — 218
27. The Big Payback — 229

Epilogue: Last Words — 234
Postscript — 236
Index — 239

ACKNOWLEDGMENTS

FROM LARRY McSHANE: First and foremost, thanks to Ralph Natale for his generosity of time and unflinching honesty during our many conversations. Special thanks also to his wife, Lucia, and the entire Natale family. Thanks to my parents, the late Nora and the still-kicking Jack McShane. Thanks to my agent, Frank Weimann, and my collaborator Dan Pearson. And thanks to those responsible for the soundtrack to this book, Philadelphia's most dynamic musical duos: Kenny Gamble & Leon Huff, Daryl Hall & John Oates, David & Serge Bielanko.

FROM DAN PEARSON: I would like to thank the people who helped shape the man Dan Pearson is today. My parents, Helene and Dan Casella, who provided a lost and tortured child with a vision for the future. Lawrence (Tumbler) Davis, who picked up the mantle and taught me how to be a man. My children, Daniel and Kristian. Daniel confirms my views that challenges can be great and that greatness can be achieved. Kristian, when I think of you, as your father,

I just smile. Ms. Donna Hylton, the sweetest toughest lady that I know. To know her is to love her. Mr. Thomas C. Harris, my right hand, and Mr. Dustin Edelhertz, my left hand. Without these people there would be no Dan Pearson!!!

Max Zampieri, dude you are so appreciated.

Thanks especially to Ralph Natale, a complex man. A man of conviction, loyalty and love of family. Ralph peeled back the onion of an America that I did not know existed. It was not for me to judge Ralph, but to listen and gather the information for his story. His family is like any other loving clan, and I'd like to thank them for providing unfettered access to Ralph and his relatives. I don't agree with all that he's done. But I came to understand why the man is the man that he is, right or wrong. Ralph Natale is Ralph Natale.

Last but never least, I would like to thank Larry McShane. What can I say, just a helluva writer!

A very special thank you to Frank Weimann who is more than just my agent but a real friend!

CAST OF CHARACTERS

A QUICK GUIDE TO THE PHILADELPHIA LA COSA NOSTRA

RALPH NATALE: Killer, union leader and organizer, head of the family from 1994–98.

ANGELO BRUNO: Family boss known as "The Docile Don," ruled peacefully for more than two decades. Murdered.

PHIL TESTA: AKA the "Chicken Man," succeeded Bruno as family boss. Murdered.

JOHN "SKINNY RAZOR" DITULLIO: Legendary mob captain and Natale's Mafia mentor.

NICKY SCARFO: Atlantic City-based Mafioso who took over the family following Testa.

JOE McGREAL: Mobbed-up South Jersey union leader. Murdered.

SALVIE TESTA: Son of Phil Testa, and widely considered the brightest star of the Philly mob's next generation. Murdered.

FRANK VADINO: Ralph's driver and right-hand man.

RONNIE TURCHI: A valued member of Ralph's crew and eventually his consigliere. Murdered.

BLINKY PALERMO: With New York mobster Frankie Carbo, he served as the mob's fixer of fights for professional boxing. A close friend and advisor for Ralph.

JOSEPH "SKINNY JOEY" MERLINO: Second-generation gangster who served as Ralph's underboss when Natale returned to Philadelphia.

MICHAEL "MIKEY CHANG" CIANCAGLINI: A member of Merlino's crew with a fearsome reputation—Ralph's favorite of the crew he assembled in Philly during the '90s. Murdered.

RAYMOND "LONG JOHN" MARTORANO: Drug dealer and partner of Angelo Bruno, eventually became a made member of the Mafia family. Murdered.

JOHN STANFA: The driver who set up Bruno for assassination, later ousted by Natale from the top of the Philly family.

CHARLIE ALLEN: Blinky Palermo's nephew, a mob hanger-on, and a federal informant.

RAYMOND BERNARD: Ralph's cousin, drug dealer—and another federal informant.

ANTHONY "TONY BANANAS" CAPONIGRO: Newark-based family consigliere under Bruno, and instigator of the plot to kill the boss. Murdered.

PETE CASELLA: Traitorous underboss who plotted against Testa.

Any man who tries to be good all the time is bound to come to ruin among the great number who are not good.

—*Niccolò Machiavelli*

Any man can take a life. But only a king can spare one.

—an old Sicilian proverb

LAST

DON

STANDING

PROLOGUE

The gifts were unwrapped and the dishes from a sumptuous holiday dinner put away at the suburban New Jersey home, a two-story colonial right off the Cooper River in Pennsauken. As the Natale family settled in front of their television to watch a yuletide special, their patriarch's mind focused on a task that was far removed from peace on earth or goodwill toward men.

Especially if that man was Joe McGreal.

Ralph Natale donned a three-quarter-length leather jacket before stepping into the darkness and heading alone toward the garage in the waning hours of Christmas Day. He marched through the breezeway toward his waiting car. He had a moment of discomfort as he pondered the task ahead on this holiest of holy days. For a minute, he thought about turning around, spending the rest of the night with his family.

Instead, he stood alone, engulfed in the solitary silence.

"For a moment," he later recalled, "I felt like I was the only human being on earth."

Natale kept walking, kept thinking, as he headed toward

the garage where his Buick Electra was parked. His mind cleared as he finally reached his destination. Natale pushed aside a fake wall to find the weapons secreted behind it and removed a pair of .38-caliber snub-nosed revolvers.

Next, he grabbed a box of hollow-point bullets and carefully loaded both weapons. One revolver went into a holster on his right ankle, the other into a deep inside pocket of his stylish coat. He opened the garage door and climbed inside the car.

He backed the Buick into the driveway, then climbed out to carefully close the garage door—intent on not disturbing his happy family. Natale reached down to touch his ankle holster, then felt for the weapon in his coat.

It was an old habit, and old habits die hard.

He put the car in gear and headed toward a cocktail lounge in the Holiday Inn opposite the racetrack in Cherry Hill. Waiting there was McGreal, a once-trusted associate in the world of La Cosa Nostra. The two were partners in the Mafia's takeover of Local 170 of the Hotel Employees and Restaurant Employees International Union. Natale, for most of his life, valued loyalty above all else. And Joe McGreal had betrayed him.

The pretense for the meeting was a Christmas shakedown of a new restaurant on the White Horse Pike in Camden County. Ralph arrived at the bar first, taking a seat with the manager, Franny McDonnel—an old friend whose presence was meant to assure McGreal this night was business as usual. Drinks were served, and drinks were downed. Then it was time for work, with Natale inviting McDonnel along for the ride.

McGreal was eager to get going: "Come on, Franny. We'll have a few drinks on the house at the new joint." As the three men walked toward McGreal's Eldorado in the lot outside, Natale noted the bulge in the right-hand pocket of the Irishman's dark cashmere overcoat. The gun bounced slightly with each stride by McGreal.

McGreal opened the driver's-side door and popped the car's locks. Natale slipped into the backseat, staking out his turf, in the spot directly behind McGreal. The bar manager grabbed the shotgun seat. They drove for twenty minutes along the Black Horse Pike toward the eatery.

As McGreal turned into the restaurant's parking lot, he sensed something wasn't right. None of the lights were on inside. "Hey, it's dark over here. What's up, Ralph?"

"Here's what's up, my friend," Natale replied.

Ralph already had one of the .38s in his right hand, and he fired directly into the back of McGreal's head. In a cruel twist apropos to the holiday, the Eldorado was a gift to the dead man just months earlier—from Ralph Natale.

1

A SIT-DOWN WITH THE BOSS

The last legitimate don of the Philadelphia family of La Cosa Nostra sits alone at a long table in a quiet room.

Ralph Natale, an integral cog in the city's organized crime scene since his teens, still exudes a bit of genial menace. Now into his eighties, he sports a runner's physique—the result of a daily morning jog, followed by a weight-lifting session. His salt-and-pepper goatee is neatly trimmed. His eyesight is failing, but his mind remains sharp as a stiletto. Dates and details spill forth as he sits beneath a knit cap, a reminder of his prison days, when Natale struggled to keep his bald head warm inside a chilly cell.

He's now four years out of prison—his second bid (mob speak for a prison sentence), thirteen years on a drug rap. The earlier stay cost Natale sixteen years, and a large chunk of his five children's lives: Lost birthdays, graduations, weddings. It was his choice: Natale could have walked free if only he chose to rat out associates such as revered Philly mob boss Angelo "the Docile Don" Bruno, his mentor and friend; legendary Chicago boss Anthony Accardo; and mob-connected union boss Ed Hanley.

He kept his mouth shut and did the time. It was the code that he'd learned and lived on the streets of South Philly. Ralph Natale was the ultimate stand-up guy, right up until the moment he sat down in a witness chair as a government witness in 2000. At that time, he became the highest-ranking Mafia member in history to turn federal witness.

The years in lockup still affect Natale in other ways. He has trouble sleeping in a bed—many nights, he leaves his wife, Lucia, alone to make himself comfortable on the couch. It feels more familiar, reminiscent of his jailhouse lodgings, as he drifts off to sleep. His bottom teeth are gone, lost to lousy prison dentistry—inmate Natale once yanked an achy tooth himself with a strand of dental floss rather than wait for a dental appointment.

And he's uncomfortable in crowds, with an hour in a room full of strangers leaving Natale disoriented after nearly three decades in the company of nobody but inmates and prison guards.

"It's what my life was," he explained. "Even before all that, I watched myself on the street. I was very wary. I watched everything and everyone. I don't like people behind me. I got threatened every day of my life. I told people, 'You know where I am. My car is parked outside. Bring it on.' Every morning I drove away from my house and I looked back in the rearview mirror. Then I made the sign of the cross.

"So far, it's worked. Look how lucky I was, to end up here."

He doesn't reflect much on his old days and his old ways, the days at the track and the nights at the bars, his days as a union boss hobnobbing with Jimmy Hoffa and the Teamsters hierarchy, the times when he had to pull the trigger or give an order to take a life.

Natale's voice turns deep and raspy as he growls about his time as a killer, when his preferred tool was a .38-caliber revolver filled with hollow-point bullets.

"Men that can kill without hesitation and it doesn't bother you, you think, 'What the hell is wrong?'" he murmurs. "But I did it. It's just some people are made that way. Not serial killers—they have no reason. If you have a reason, you get it done with, fuck it. Go have a drink somewhere. Maybe today brings something else."

He would eventually confess to killing McGreal and another man and acknowledge his role in six more murders during a bloody Philadelphia mob war involving his long-shot ascension to head of the local Mafia family—the apex of a five-decade run in "The Life." But word on the South Philly streets linked Natale to mob murder and menace far beyond those eight deaths.

He shrugs when recalling those days.

"When McGreal got killed, the next morning—'It was Ralphy!'" he said. "Somebody got killed in Detroit—that was Ralphy. Meanwhile, I was in Philadelphia. I used to laugh. But it was good for the reputation."

Even now, he takes pride in his efficient lethal work and shows no remorse for anything.

"It's not that I take pleasure in it," he explains. "I never take pleasure in killing anybody. I tell you, when it comes to that there, I kill 'em so fast they don't even know they're dead. I shoot 'em. Right in the face."

But his rise from a kid shuffling betting slips in South Philly bars in the 1940s to point man for the mob's infiltration of Atlantic City in the sixties and seventies to the don of the Philadelphia mob in the 1990s was defined as much by the men he spared as those he killed. Natale's decisions to let mob associates Charlie Allen and Ron Previte keep breathing—made nearly two decades apart—twice landed him behind bars for double-digit jail terms. And a direct order from boss Angelo Bruno stopped him from killing the treacherous and bloodthirsty Atlantic City mobster Nicky Scarfo, a choice that proved disastrous for the entire Philadelphia mob family after decades of peace and prosperity under Natale's friend the Docile Don.

"Pinpoints in time," he now observes with the detachment of hindsight. Life is often about karma and the ever-widening ripples set in motion by a single choice, an ill-chosen word, or the holstering of a handgun. Death can come from a simple hand gesture, a nod of the head, a roll of the eyes.

"No matter how insignificant they appear at the time they occur, these things can determine a man's life until there is no more," Natale says.

Atlantic City—viewed as a Garden of Eden for greedy Philadelphia mobsters once gambling was legalized—became a recurring theme that ran through much of his life. Natale was there for the mob's initial plans to seize control of the casino unions. He stewed behind bars as mob rival "Little Nicky" Scarfo ruined the Philly family and threatened to interrupt the flow of cash from the Jersey Shore. And Natale returned to his hometown from jail determined to reclaim the prize.

Ralph Natale spent twenty-nine years of his adult life in jail. The first stretch was a direct result of another Natale decision: he was no rat. Promises of early parole, lonely years apart from his wife and growing family, a poisonous anger that grew as he felt the betrayal of his fellow mafiosi—nothing could convince Natale to flip and work for the feds.

Until he finally did.

There are things he misses about the mob life, the pumping adrenaline and the high-wire tension of day-to-day life outside the law. It was a man's world: good men and bad men, killers and thieves, bosses and capos. At one time, men of honor and respect. Later, men considered punks and pretenders by Natale.

This was his world for most of five decades.

"You walk into a room, and you know something's gonna happen," he says of those days. "What I see in somebody's face, what they see and what they're looking at. Or you're walking with somebody, and you know in your heart of hearts he wants to kill you. And you're thinking, 'I'm gonna kill him as soon as I can.'

"I want you to understand I'm not a maniac or a mob serial killer. I never touched an innocent person in my life. I never touched a woman, or a child. Or a man trying to make a living for his family. I can say that 'cause that's what I am. But you fuck with me, you're gonna have a problem.

"Some men are that way. I was that way. That's what it is."

Natale explains what he means with a pop culture reference, quoting from a Quentin Tarantino movie.

"Did you ever see the movie *Kill Bill,* when David Carradine and Uma Thurman are fighting at the end, and he shoots her with the truth serum, and they're talking? He says, 'You know, you're a born killer, and that's what you'll always be.'

"And I'm a killer, too."

Natale is adamant about one other thing: his story is the one true tale of the rise and fall of the family that he twice swore an oath of lifelong loyalty and silence to serve and protect.

"It's the real Mafia story—no bullshit," he declares. "When that guy Mario Puzo wrote *The Godfather,* he had a lot of friends in different families. They told him little episodes. He wasn't there, but he finally put it all together."

And then Ralph Natale starts to speak.

2

Ralph Natale was born hard.

The son of the unforgiving South Philadelphia streets arrived on March 6, 1935, brought home by a tough-guy father and a mother with few maternal instincts in the hard times of the Great Depression. Ralph was the older of two sons born five years apart; his parents were the first generation of their families born in the United States after his four grandparents had emigrated from Italy to the City of Brotherly Love.

His paternal grandparents died two weeks apart during the 1918 flu pandemic that ravaged the city's Italian neighborhood. An estimated 30 million people died worldwide, with twelve thousand killed in Philadelphia as its tiny morgue was overrun with corpses. People struck by the killer bug were moved from their beds into wooden coffins even before taking their last breaths as the disease spread.

The coffins were then stacked on street corners, where they were loaded in bulk on flatbed trucks and taken away.

Josephine Ianelli Natale went first, believing that her

husband, Ralph, would survive to raise their three children: twelve-year-old Michael, eight-year-old Sammy, and the baby, five-year-old Grace.

But Ralph had already contracted the deadly disease, and he joined his immigrant wife inside the coffins on the sidewalks of South Philly. The three kids were left on their own, and life as an orphan exerted a profound effect on the eldest son, Michael.

"My father never knew a love or kindness from a mother or a father," Ralph recalled. "So how was he to know how to give this to a son? Not a word of kindness or a simple touch of love from either mother or father since I was old enough to remember. They were never, 'You're gonna be okay, this and that.' Never once!"

Michael Natale became known on the street as Spike. His sons Michael Jr. and Ralphy, a pair of peas from different pods, grew up in two different worlds inside the same home. Michael Jr. was artistic, sensitive. And Ralphy was becoming Ralph. "He was so different from me," Natale said. "He really was."

The lack of a kind, loving home emotionally crippled young Ralph, whose moral compass went askew before puberty. He found himself devoid of good feelings, cold-blooded and predatory in his approach to life.

"What made me this way?" he mused decades later about the arc of his life. "I never knew what love was in that house. They were always fighting, always angry. And I said, 'Oh, that's where it's at. If that's where it's at, that's what life's gonna be for me. And I went that way. And I prayed for their souls, that they would be in peace."

Spike worked as a pickup man for the Philly mob, collecting betting slips around town from assorted Mafia-backed businesses. He collected clips left at the counters of candy stores or stuffed inside pipes in back alleys. Spike never owned a car and was seen daily making his rounds on foot through the local streets, ultimately delivering the paperwork to a pal named Sparky. Spike wound up doing a bit of time at Eastern State Penitentiary.

His slender frame didn't carry much weight—just 125 pounds, although he toted a .45-caliber pistol "that weighed more than he did," Natale recalled. "But a tough guy. Tough." Spike also ran a numbers business in the black section of South Philly, off South Street.

The only bit of childhood bonding between father and eldest son was the day when Spike taught his boy how to fire a gun.

"I shot his .45. He took me down on the waterfront and said, 'Hold it with both hands,'" Natale said. "*Boom!* They were like cannons."

The first time Natale felt the homicidal rage that would become so familiar in the future came one night at age twelve, when he violated his father's strict 9:00 p.m. curfew. The boy lost track of time and returned home to find his dad waiting at the front door. He still remembers the first words out of the old man's mouth—and everything that followed.

"Son of a bitch, I told you," said Spike before planting a hard kick with the side of his foot on the youngster. Ralph's reaction seemed to come from nowhere and consume his entire consciousness, like some long-hidden instinct just now bubbling to the surface. He went from humiliated to infuriated in seconds.

The life-changing boot still stings all these decades later.

"It would have been better if he smacked me or punched me in the face," Natale remembers. "But that's like I was scum—you kick somebody that way. I turned around, I said, 'Don't you ever touch me again. And don't you ever think about doing what you just did again.'

"I have to tell you, if I had something in my hands, I would have killed him. That's when I knew what I was. Twelve years old. The truth, I mean it. I wouldn't let no-body touch me like that again. Nobody. It's there. It's always there."

Outside the house, the Philly kid did his best to find a safe place. He served as the undersized-if-athletic catcher on a youth league team that won the city Police Athletic League title, where third-grader Natale was coached by a pair of Philly cops. "I was good ballplayer, and it's not bragging," said Natale, who played catcher when none of the other kids wanted to wear the so-called tools of ignorance.

But it was his father's mob cohorts who appealed to the youth, already envisioning a crooked future in grammar school. Spike provided his son's entrée to the underworld, enlisting the preteen to handle a collection from a black bar owner named George Wallace.

Like father, like son: Spike told Ralphy that he should travel on foot. And so the young Natale marched through the black section of the city on his mission.

"He knew that I knew how to handle myself," Natale recalled of his first taste of illegal business. "He told me, 'Just be careful, and do what you gotta do, 'cause you're walking through a tough neighborhood.' But a lot of the black kids went to school with me. They knew who I was. They knew they might get me now—but if you did, you'd better leave your neighborhood, 'cause if I'm alive, I'm gonna come back.

"That was the reputation I had at eleven years old."

The youth headed to Wallace's home and knocked on the

door of the address provided by Spike. A woman answered, looked at the little white kid, and asked what he wanted. Ralphy politely replied that his father had dispatched him to see Mr. Wallace.

"She smiled. I was the most respectful little son of a bitch," Natale says with a smile. "I really was. She said, 'Okay, he's not here. He's at the bar over on the corner. You want to come in here and wait for him?' I said, 'I can't come in.'"

When Mrs. Wallace asked why, the boy provided a ready answer: "Your man is over there. He's not here."

The adult Natale laughs in retelling the tale. "She loved that! That's how I was when I was a boy. She sent me over to the Budweiser Bar. I opened the door, the jukebox is going, and there's a voice: 'What do you want here, boy? Are you Spike's son?'

"I said yes, and he told me to come over. I said, 'You're Mr. Wallace?' He laughed: 'Oh, you're checking me out? Come with me.' We went into the men's room, and he gives me the sheet. He says, 'How did you get up here?' Well, I walked. He said, 'You got a lot of balls. I'm gonna give you a lot of money, too.'"

The diminutive bagman's reply was succinct: "I don't care. I'm supposed to come up and see you. I didn't know what you were gonna give me."

Wallace laughed and asked if Ralphy wanted anything from the bar before the long walk home.

"I don't drink," the youngster replied.

Wallace never forget his exchange with the well-mannered boy and never failed to bring it up when they crossed paths during Ralph's ensuing ascension to the upper echelons of organized crime.

Just as the kick had galvanized Natale's outlook on life,

the trip cemented his plans for the future: "I was eleven years old, and I thought, 'This is it.' There was no hesitation. I never hesitated. I wish I had sometimes. When somebody pulled out a pistol, it didn't bother me, 'cause that's what you had to do at that time.

"I learned what those kind of men said: 'If you don't step up, you're gonna be left behind.' If somebody said, 'Let's go,' you'd better get up. You can't hesitate. And to step up, I was always first."

Despite his troubled home life, young Ralphy excelled in school. The bright young student was quick to raise his hand in class, much to the delight of his second-grade teacher. He was particularly adept at reading comprehension, retaining details and descriptions almost instantaneously.

The brightest students were often allowed to skip a grade, and he was moved directly from the second grade into the fourth—and then again, from the fourth to the sixth.

Natale, in class with kids two and three years older, became less comfortable and less interested in education. A junior high school IQ test nevertheless confirmed that Ralphy was among the sharpest students in his grade, and Natale recalled hearing the results from a teacher—a 138, a ranking of superior intelligence.

"Mr. Horowitz told me I had one of the highest scores that he'd ever seen," said Natale. "According to Mr. Horowitz, I coulda been anything I wanted to be. But who's gonna tell me about being anything else but what I was, if I'm that way already, like I was?"

Natale was thrown out of Southern at age fourteen, the second high school to banish him. And so began the real education of Ralph Natale, with classes conducted across South Philadelphia: in the streets, in the bars, and in the humidor of Yahn & McCormick, South Philly's biggest cigar store.

"I love South Philly," he recalled wistfully. "I love the people in South Philly. I love the air. I love the scent and aroma of different cooking. I see a woman, walking and pushing a cart—I enjoy that. That's my family. That's where I was born and raised."

His favorite spot was always the Italian Market, a retail center unlike any other in the city. Cheese shops stood with fruit and vegetable stores, alongside fish markets and butchers' shops where live animals were killed and sold. The streets were filled with tantalizing scents. Passersby enjoyed free samples of the homemade cheese and Sicilian-style black olives sprinkled with red seed pepper.

Here, amid the hustle and bustle and constant commerce, a young immigrant named Phil Testa made a living selling chickens. A strange combination of good luck and bad fortune would eventually lead him to the top position of the Philly mob—for a mere twelve months.

3

Aspiring mobster Natale was fifteen when a pal convinced him to leave the neighborhood for a Friday-night dance at a nearby church. The pair had played in a sandlot football game earlier in the day, with Natale breaking his nose while making a tackle. In addition to his one and only suit, a well-worn blue number, the teen sported a pair of nascent black eyes. The suit was so shiny from repeated trips to the dry cleaner that "it looked like it would shatter if I fell."

The young Romeo donned a white shirt and his lone tie for the trip, enticed by his pal Bucky's pitch: "He said, 'C'mon, I heard there's pretty girls from above Broad Street.' And those girls didn't swear. In my neighborhood, there were nice girls, but they'd fistfight with you and call you 'motherfucker' this and that. I said, 'I don't feel like going.'

"He finally talked me into it. And that's where I met my wife."

Natale spied eighteen-year-old Lucia from across the dance floor and resolved to make his move. The nervous young suitor asked for a dance, but there was a problem: He didn't know a single step. The beautiful older woman, who worked as a dressmaker in a South Philly business, also noticed that Ralph looked a little younger than his declared age of eighteen.

But love won out: Ralph walked her home and asked for her phone number.

"I never forgot it from that day: Fulton 9-4326," he declared. "She said, 'You gotta write that down.' I said, 'I don't have to write your number down. I'll remember.' Oh, I came up with some lines!"

Their courtship was quick, as the underage Natale—without a driver's license—borrowed cars from older guys to take her on dates. Lucia finally told Ralph that she knew he was just sixteen, but they were young and in love and it didn't much matter. On one of their dates, she broke the news to Ralphy: she was pregnant.

He was sixteen and about to become a father. And, it turned out, a husband. Once again, he never hesitated:

"I said, 'Let's get married,' because I loved her. I loved her no matter what I did. . . . And I still love her deeply."

The teenaged couple, after welcoming their first son, found a small apartment to raise their family. Natale, despite his tender age and inexperience, was an up-and-comer in the world of the Philadelphia mob. His first concern remained constant: providing for his wife and kids, by any means necessary.

"I would do anything. I liked to work," Natale recalled. "We didn't have much, but we started to move up a little bit. And I always did every little thing."

In the fall of 1955, Natale fenced some stolen goods, turned a quick profit, and decided it was time to go see his favorite ballplayer: New York Yankees center fielder Mickey

Mantle. The Bronx Bombers were facing the Brooklyn Dodgers in the World Series, and Natale turned his cash into two tickets for Game Three at Ebbets Field.

By then, the couple had welcomed a second son.

"I told my wife, 'Can your mother watch the kids?'" he remembered with a smile decades later. "I got seats out in right-center field, and we watched. I said, 'Don't worry—the Mick is gonna hit one out.' The next inning, he hit a tremendous homer. What a time that was to go to New York!"

The young couple bought a pair of souvenir minibats, each inscribed with Mantle's name, to bring back for their boys.

Though Natale found himself naturally attracted to the older mobsters who mentored the young thug, he still bristles at the suggestion that he was in search of a substitute father.

"I'm far from that stereotype," he said flatly. "That ain't me, not in a million years. I don't need no father. My father was a strong man. But he was not my father to me. I mean, I came from his seed. But he was not my father.

"I am what I am. I just wanted to get ahead for my wife and children, to give them something."

His decision to join the Mafia came as no surprise to his large extended family, which included his mother's nine siblings. "They were proud of me!" he declared. "They knew me since I was a boy. And they told people, 'You fuck around in my neighborhood, I'll call my nephew!'"

The Natales eventually landed in Southwest Philly, a predominantly Irish neighborhood. Natale's young family was the only Italian one on the block, and that suited him just fine. He didn't want his own kids exposed to the toxic lures of the old neighborhood.

"I had to move out of South Philly," he says now. "I thought, 'If my sons grow up to be like me, I'll get sick. Sick."

Their new home came their way through the help of young Ralph's capo, legendary local mob killer John "Skinny Razor" DiTullio, a veteran of the infamous Philly mob war with the Lanzetti brothers before Ralphy was born.

DiTullio was one of ten kids, a typically expansive Italian brood struggling to make ends meet. Food was often leftovers or vegetables with no meat. He stuffed cardboard in the soles of his shoes to keep water from leaking through the holes. And he made his bones in the mob killing of opera great Mario Lanza's nephew.

His nickname came from his weapon of choice, a thin, sharp blade typically secreted in the jacket pocket of his suit. DiTullio's mob lineage was impeccable; the old-timer once had a face-to-face meeting with Al Capone, who expressed admiration for DiTullio's killing skills during the Philly infighting of the twenties and thirties.

"Eighteen, nineteen years old—he already had a reputation, forget about it," Natale says with admiration. "Capone shook his hand—he told me this, one night, over Scotch. And he told Skinny, 'There are certain people, a year from now, they're not gonna be around because of you.'

"Skinny said, 'Oh, I felt so good.' Like he graduated summa cum laude!"

The precocious Natale earned his own street cred before he was old enough to legally drive or buy a drink. DiTullio knew Natale's dad, Spike, from the numbers-running job and took notice of the up-and-comer. The Razor saw a bright future for the teenage hoodlum.

"I was starting to make a reputation as a young lad, much faster than anybody ever thought," Natale remembered of those days. "And Skinny sent for me—I musta been maybe fourteen. There was an after-hours place on Eighth Street, right below Washington Avenue, and a lot of the made guys used to go there late at night. Skinny had me sitting down in there.

"He gave me the look—he had a face like a Tatar, one of those old Mongolians. So I stand up, and he says, 'Ralphy, come over here.' I wouldn't dare sit down. He said, 'You know Mr. Bruno, of course.'"

"Hello, Mr. Bruno," the kid replied.

"I was gonna put my hand out, but I stopped," Natale said of this pivotal get-together. "You learn things by being around—you don't offer your hand to a boss. That's crude. So I waited, and he put his hand out."

Then Bruno spoke: "I heard a lot of good things about you, Ralphy."

Natale offered a quick response: "I will never let you hear anything bad about me."

Natale recalled wistfully, "He liked that. He said, 'I know your father. He's a good man, and we expect a lot from you, and so does this man here, Skinny."

"Thank you," the awestruck teen replied. "It's an honor to meet you this way."

"Okay," Bruno replied before sending the teen on his way. "We'll talk someday."

Hard case DiTullio developed an instant soft spot for the young Natale, providing a master's class in the Mafia to his young and ambitious charge. His classroom was the Friendly Tavern on South Eighth Street, where Natale proved a particularly apt pupil.

"That was the start," Natale says now. "He took time out of his life to teach me about what you had to be to be somebody in the family. And he knew I had it. I grew up knowing him. Skinny Razor—he helped all the people in the Italian Market. They loved him. He helped them with all their problems, any problem. You do something wrong to them, you're gonna go. He ain't gonna play games."

Natale, when not on the street, worked a few night shifts behind the stick at the Friendly. DiTullio made sure that he got paid for both.

"There's no training program like they do in a big company," he explained of his on-the-job training with Skinny. "When Skinny's there, everybody knew it in the city. That meant he condoned everything that I did before, and you'd better watch out, 'cause I had that license now. And that's how it happened."

And Ralphy paid attention: "I studied men for a long time. Even when I was a little boy, I was always a people watcher. Always."

DiTullio admired Natale's don't-give-a-damn approach to life, going balls to the walls without worries about the fallout and taking responsibility for his actions.

"I never was a con artist," said Natale. "I never gave a fuck who liked me. That's my life. Skinny loved that more than anybody. Skinny had a little Louie Prima in his voice, he used to say, 'Man, you don't care who likes ya, do ya?'

"And I said," Natale recounted with a loud laugh, " 'As long as you like me.' "

DiTullio's survived the local war for control of the mob between the old school Mustache Petes of Sicily and the American-born Young Turks eager to make the family their own. Though himself born in Philly, Skinny Razor was brutally instrumental in keeping the old guard in control.

The young Razor's take-no-prisoners crew included the

legendary Harry "the Hunchback" Riccobene and future capo Freddie Iezzi. Natale offered a poetic appraisal of his friend and mentor: "Skinny Razor was to the Philadelphia La Cosa Nostra what the Great Wall of China was to the enemies of that vast empire."

If you were Skinny Razor's friend, you had a friend for life. And if you were his enemy, that life would be considerably shortened. "We had more arms than an armory under the bar," Natale recalled.

DiTullio's way of handling mob business provided Natale with a template for his own career. He wasn't flashy and never did anything for show. Killing was for business, period. Your reputation speaks for itself; there's no reason to go shouting from the rooftops about anything related to the family or your part in it.

"I never tried to impress anybody in my life," says Natale. "Maybe when I talked and said things, people responded in a certain way. That's on them. Maybe they got dirty underwear. That's the old saying in the mob—if you don't show up, you got dirty underwear. In other words, you did something wrong. If they make a mistake, they gotta go. You gotta go sometime. You know the old saying: everybody dies."

Natale, as his financial status improved, started dressing in style. He favored tailor-made shirts with a barrel sleeve and double buttons, a nice suit, nothing gaudy, no jewelry, and a hint of cologne.

Natale bought into the mob ethos without hesitation, and the Philadelphia family quickly became the epicenter of his existence. He looks back on that choice without regret: "At that time in my life, with those kind of men, it meant more than anything. It meant my whole life. It meant more than

my family, because my family will benefit from me being
what I am. I didn't have anything. I didn't know anything. I
didn't have a formal education. I didn't have a trade. I didn't
have nothing.

"All I had was me. At that time, I weighed 140 pounds.
That's all I had! But I knew what I was. And I didn't fear anything in the world. If you die, at least you die good—'Hey,
I'm somebody!' And that's what you feel. And that's what I
felt. Just being near that circle of power makes you something
better."

The illegal money was good, but Natale still looked forward to the nights when DiTullio handed him a pay envelope
after a night of pouring drinks. When the bar closed, the
lights and the jukebox were turned down low and the two
men sat and talked about life to a musical backdrop of Ella
Fitzgerald and Billy Eckstine.

DiTullio did the talking, and Natale listened.

"I'd say, 'What's the matter? You got something on your
mind?' And he say, 'No, I just wanna talk.' Sometimes we'd
sit for two, three hours, sip our Scotch, and talk about everything—people and life. You'd be surprised the things I
learned from him about people, so-called tough guys and the
mob and this and that. I learned you were a gentleman toward
other men and women. And I learned that in this world, there
are motherfuckers that you cannot be good to. I'm not talking
about criminality. I'm talking about life."

Sitting there one night over a glass of good booze, he
heard the sad tale of Harry Barry—a fake tough guy with
a phony name. He dressed the part and talked the talk and
downed the drinks. In the world of Texas ranchers, there's an
expression for guys like that: *big hat, no cattle.*

There's a name for them in South Philly, too: *asshole*.

The tale was told by Joe Panisi, the bookie who handled all the bar's betting action.

One night in the early 1940s, Barry bopped into a Jersey nightclub with a camel-hair coat and an attitude. The rest of the clientele included Philly bigwig and future boss Marco Reginelli and his crew.

"Those days, Italians would act like they weren't Italians," Natale explained of Barry's adopted surname. "All the fighters became Irish, different names. All the guys used to go there, eat and drink and this and that. Harry Barry's dressed nice, acting like a dangerous guy. He goes into the bathroom, and the guy who comes in behind him is Marty Martell, the bodyguard of Marco. An old fighter. He says, 'You know Harry, why don't you come over and say hello to the boss over there?'

"Harry Barry gets snotty when he drinks: 'What the fuck do I care? I do what I want to do.'

"Harry carried a razor like Skinny did, in his suit pocket, covered with a handkerchief. Pulled it out, zoom! He opened Martell's whole face up. Blood all over. Then he spit on him and walked out. He carried that scar for his whole life."

Word quickly leaked back to DiTullio about Barry's insolence toward Reginelli and the attack on Martell. The mobster frowned at the idea of people disrespecting his friends and was keeping an eye out for Barry when his target walked into the Friendly Tavern with a pal.

Barry was looking for Panisi, a gambling savant who kept all his records—point spreads, wins, losses, debts unpaid—in his head. DiTullio and Panisi were sitting at the bar having a drink.

DiTullio leaned over and asked the bookie about Barry's

gambling habits. He was betting big, said Panisi, and was currently a week behind in making good.

"Skinny says into Panisi's ear, 'You'd better collect tonight,'" recalled Natale. "The next morning, I was in George Washington Elementary School. There's a crowd around. They said, 'Somebody's laying over there! The cops are there!' Harry Barry's laying against the steps of a row house, and he's dead. Years later, I found out about it because I became somebody.

"And Panisi—he was a good friend of my father, too—says, 'I'm gonna make you laugh with this one: "You'd better collect your money tonight!"'"

4

"Where are we going?"

A twenty-year-old Ralph Natale asked the question, unsure if he would get an answer.

"Just drive north," said his lone passenger, Angelo Bruno, a revered top-level mafioso and Ralph's mob patron. "To the Holland Tunnel and Little Italy in Manhattan."

Ralphy, who had recently started chauffeuring the boss, started the car and headed silently toward the New Jersey Turnpike.

"He would have all these kiss asses drive for him," Natale said. "And he said, one time, 'Maybe later this week I'm gonna go somewhere. You come pick me up in the morning.' What he liked about me was I didn't talk too much."

The long, quiet round-trip wound resonate for Natale in the years ahead, changing forever the arc of his life and his career.

"We went to a nice little social club in the Italian section of Manhattan," said Natale. "He gets out, and all the men sitting outside get up. He told me, 'Stay out here. I'm gonna say hello to somebody in there, and then we're gonna go to a hotel."

Ralphy, in a sports coat and dress slacks, was ready for anything: "I knew when you went to New York, look proper."

Bruno emerged and began dictating directions to the hotel; they headed uptown until they arrived at their destination: the Waldorf Astoria Hotel.

Natale was stunned. "I thought, 'What the fuck is he going to the Waldorf Astoria for?' We pulled up to the side entrance, not the front. He says, 'Okay, put the car there.' They had people out there waiting to take my car. Me and Ang went in, past the Peacock Alley—the bar. The Waldorf Astoria, Jesus Christ. It was funny. And he said, 'Okay, sit outside. Don't go in the bar.'

"I gave him the look: I know better than that. I wouldn't breathe if he didn't tell me it was okay. So I sat down and waited. The waitress came over: 'What do you want, young man?' I got a club soda with a slice of lemon. Of course, she knew who I was with."

The ritzy Park Avenue hotel held a special place in mob lore. Founding father Charles "Lucky" Luciano kept a suite in the Waldorf Towers for years, apartment 39C, paying $800 a month. The Mafia's ties to the Waldorf continued long after Luciano was deported; the spacious suite was now leased year-round for use by the Commission and its members, using the name of a small Queens real estate business. Its owner's parents had lived next door to mob boss Carlo Gambino's cousins in Sicily.

"The Commission used to meet there in the Waldorf. They had a set of rooms under a phony name," Natale recalled. "They kept that place for years, and nobody knew."

Natale recalled waiting alone for two hours, silent and unsure of what was going on. He was starting to get antsy when the elevator doors opened. Bruno exited, but he wasn't alone. Ralphy recognized the second man instantly.

"Carlo Gambino," Natale says of his first encounter with capo di tutt'i capi, the powerful boss of the nation's most powerful mob family. "My God. I come to attention. I went over. I didn't come right up because that's improper. Angelo says, 'Come here, say hello to Mr. Gambino.' He puts his hand out, and he shakes my hand—firm.

"I looked at this face, and he looked me straight in the eye: 'I hear many good things about you.'"

The two bosses from either end of New Jersey were close friends who once hailed from the same hometown in Sicily. Bruno arrived after Gambino, who helped introduce his old friend to the ways of this new world across the Atlantic. Natale recalls the pair as kindred spirits, men of unusual dignity, class, and honor:

"They weren't men like John Gotti, the type of guy who walks in: 'Look at me!' Neither one of them. You could sense these were men of substance. Angelo adopted the spirit and the manner of Carlo Gambino. Carlo was like an older brother to Angelo. Over the years, they shared different things—legal and illegal."

The two dons walked back outside, with Natale trailing at a respectful distance. Bruno's car was already waiting at the curb.

"I'm bewildered," Natale remembered. "Do they own this place? The waiters knew Gambino. The people at the desk knew him. Ang climbed into the car right away. He was a chain-smoker, so I'd have the window open. We start driving."

The ride south was dead silent, with Natale behind the wheel. It wasn't his place to say anything, and so he said nothing. The boss lit cigarette after endless cigarette, the smoke wafting out a window opened just a crack. "He smoked so much, I thought I was gonna get cancer," said Natale.

Bruno finally broke the hush. "Do you know what that means when that man says that to you?" he asked, a serious look across his face.

"Yes, I do," Natale replied. "And I will always remember that."

Bruno looked directly at his young associate, his eyes turning soft. Natale, despite a childhood devoid of such attention from his own father, recognized the unspoken message of paternal concern on the Philadelphia boss's face.

"There are ways—men of power have a look that tells you, 'We're talking to you, but don't think we're friendly here," Natale said. "But when they soften their eyes: 'I care for you. I'm looking out for you, like a son.'"

Natale remembered this trip for the rest of his life, and years later his respectful demeanor and boss's support would catapult him into the upper echelon of the mob.

Natale crossed paths with the New York City boss at a second meeting. Just as he had at the Waldorf, young Ralphy impressed the older man—who kept the memory with him for years, until the day when he decided the kid from Philly was just the man he needed for a major mob undertaking.

5

THE RISE OF THE DOCILE DON

Angelo Bruno, the man who became known as the Docile Don, assumed command of the Philadelphia Mafia family in a fashion befitting his nickname: no shooting, no killing, just a peaceful ascension after a successful career. Bruno, after his installation by the mob's ruling Commission, spared the life of his rival for the post to earn his nickname of tranquillity.

Earlier Philly management changes had come in more spectacular fashion: John Avena was gunned down in the street back in 1936. Things were different when word of boss Marco Reginelli's 1956 death from pancreatic cancer reached the South Philly bars owned and frequented by the city's Mafia.

The future of each and every one depended on the choice of the new padrone.

The Sicilian-born Bruno was the popular choice, but one of only three candidates for the top spot in the late 1950s. One was Skinny Razor, who opted for his golf game and his bar business over the headaches of running the family. In mob parlance, DiTullio didn't have the time or inclination to sit with every guy walking into his bar, hat in hand.

The other was Joe Ida, already part of the family's ruling elite. But Natale says there was little question that Bruno was the man for the job: "It's simple—he ran the business end when he was a capo. He ran the street. Honest to a fault. Loyal? Beyond that. Everything was right. If the money was supposed to be here, it would be here."

Bruno's candidacy was boosted by his close ties to Gambino, the head of the New York crime family that bore his name into the new millennium. The pair followed similar career paths in the two East Coast cities—with one major exception: Gambino's ascension to the seat of power followed the brutal murder of Albert Anastasia. Bruno would take a different approach.

Ida had different ideas about Reginelli's replacement. No one, the treacherous mobster decided, was better for the job than Joe Ida.

The selection process was simple: The Philly capos would vote on their choice for the new boss. Their pick would be sent to New York to the Commission, the heads of the five Big Apple families. The final decision was theirs.

Ida decided to fix the election by killing his top competition, Angelo Bruno. "Jealousy, ego, and greed," said Natale of Ida's twisted mind-set. Within hours of Reginelli's death, Ida reached out to a Naples-born shooter named Ignazio Dante and laid out his plot inside the latter's small casino operation on Christian Street. Dante, who had fought alongside DiTullio in the earlier mob war, was promised a higher-ranking family position and a percentage of its illegal income for his cooperation.

But Ida had failed to do his homework. When Dante had

wanted to retire from the mob's cutthroat world, Bruno had swayed the bosses to set him free. His small casino operated with the full approval of the Philadelphia family.

"Normally," noted Natale, "a retirement for a soldier of the Mafia is not followed by a Social Security check, but by a hearse." Bruno had insured Dante would live long and prosper. And now, as befitting the owner of a gambling operation, he would repay his benefactor in spades.

Dante made a beeline for a no-frills Italian restaurant called Corona di Ferra, a compact eatery with a distinctive floor fashioned from diamond-shaped black and white tiles. The same men always seemed to occupy the same half dozen tables near the bar, but Dante wanted to see the man seated in the main dining room up three steps from the entrance.

Angelo Bruno was holding court, with members of his crew at the surrounding tables. Dante respectfully inquired if he should wait at the bar or head inside to speak with Bruno.

"He hasn't ordered yet, so do what you please," responded the manager.

Dante made his way slowly toward the dining room, offering a smile as he caught the attention of one of Bruno's dinner guests. The guest returned the smile, and Bruno turned to see what prompted the grin. When he spied Dante, the capo offered his own warm smile of greeting.

"Ignazio, here, take a chair," said Bruno.

Dante, using the seat only to brace himself, instead leaned down and whispered into Bruno's ear, "I must speak to you alone. It's a matter of the most serious of things." Bruno told his old friend by the elbow and headed toward the front, with the mafiosi standing in a sign of respect as the two walked out the door for a walk around the block.

The pair were now arm in arm, walking almost as one, while Dante laid bare the murder plot proposed by Ida. As Natale heard it, Bruno's face remained a blank slate—not a flash of anger nor a hint of disappointment. The two men walked back to the restaurant, where Dante offered an apology to Bruno's table for his interruption.

"I'll get back to you," promised Bruno, who then offered his own apology and made an exit, pleading a sudden emergency. A phone call was placed to Gambino in New York, and Bruno—with capo Freddie Iezzi at the wheel—was on his way to the city within the hour. They headed to the Waldorf, where New York's bosses awaited.

Bruno shared the details and received their approval to give Ida what's known as the eternal nap. Instead, the new boss—approved now by the nation's five most powerful bosses as the successor to Reginelli—returned to Philadelphia and gave his would-be killer a pass. Joe Ida was deported in 1959, and Angelo Bruno earned his oxymoronic nom de Mafia by sparing his life.

There was one other change. The South Jersey faction of the Philadelphia family would report to Bruno from now on, a change from the old days when the city and its suburbs answered to two different leaders. Bruno was already showing one of the main attributes for successfully running a family: insuring its stability in times of unrest.

Before leaving the Waldorf, Gambino pulled Bruno aside for a short primer on his new life as a don. The two sat at a table, a plate of the Waldorf's finest china filled with biscotti and espresso between them, as Gambino explained that job one was choosing the right underboss. The two spoke in Sicilian, like a father advising his son. Bruno lit a cigarette as he listened intently to the advice.

Choose someone without ties to anyone else, Gambino declared, without a history that might cloud the vision that Bruno would impart about the Philadelphia family. "You must be his mentor in all things, so only you can show him us," Gambino explained. "Only you can impart what you want him and your family to feel about La Cosa Nostra. This is most important."

Bruno headed back to Philadelphia with the advice already ingrained into his thoughts going forward.

Bruno had Iezzi drive him directly to the Friendly Tavern, where he would share the news of his good fortune with Skinny Razor—his friend and fellow traveler through the Life since both were nineteen. Bruno's decision only reinforced to Iezzi that New York had made the right choice.

"The smart move, according to Sicilian philosophy, is when forming a family of your own you must first align yourself with the strongest capos as your foundation," Natale explained. "Ang's decision told everybody in the family that there would be no dissent over New York's decision. And it would also make anyone think twice about opposing the decision, given Skinny's expertise in making people disappear."

Iezzi, a DiTullio pal since the old mob war, didn't need directions. The driver parked on Washington Street, near the front entrance to the bar. Skinny's personal bodyguard, Lefty Gatti, heard the sound of an engine and bolted immediately toward the front door as Iezzi exited the Lincoln Town Car.

"You know what to do," said Bruno—and after a lifetime of knowing what to do, Iezzi headed toward the front door. "I'll wait by the side door," Bruno added before slipping away.

What happened next was instructive: While many bosses

like to make an ostentatious entrance, basking in the love and fear of their minions, Bruno had an aversion to such grandstanding. So on the night of his ascension, the humble Bruno opted for a back entrance to the bar.

"He held himself with dignity and humility as he should, coming to tell a man who could easily have been as honored as he was," Natale recalled. Iezzi went in through the front, looking for DiTullio. Gatti greeted him warmly, with a smile and a handshake. DiTullio saw the pair and waved to Iezzi to join him at the bar. Iezzi asked quietly if Gatti could open the side door, because Angelo Bruno was waiting outside. DiTullio took the keys and stood up: "I'll let my friend in myself." The two men embraced wordlessly, and with one look, each knew exactly how their upcoming conversation would play out. No rancor or jealousy or treachery was in either one's mind. It was a moment of triumph and joy for the family and the two old friends.

A bar patron pumping money into the jukebox first noticed Bruno's arrival. By the time the new don and Skinny Razor walked toward the table in the farthest end of the bar, everyone inside was staring at the two revered mobsters. Then they stood in a show of respect as Bruno offered a wave with his left arm.

Bruno rarely drank in public, occasionally enjoying a cocktail while out with his wife, his capos, and their wives at a Thursday-night dinner that became a family tradition under the Docile Don. But on this night, he ordered a Canadian Club straight up, with Pellegrino water on the side. He then bought the bar a round before leaning over to speak with DiTullio in a low whisper.

"John," said the new boss, "you are the first to know in Philadelphia. We've just come back from New York, and the

Commission named me as Marco's successor and has combined us all together—South Jersey with us. We're all under one flag."

DiTullio rose to his feet, raising his glass of Scotch high to pledge his allegiance. It was an oath that the old warrior took more seriously than anything else in his life.

"I am yours, and my entire crew is yours to command," he announced. "It will be so until I die. *Salute!*"

Now Bruno stood, kissing his trusted capo on the cheek. "I'm honored to have your loyalty, your life, and the lives of all of your men."

Bruno became the kind of boss who made regular visits to long-retired "Don Turridu" Sabella with free cartons of cigarettes and other gifts. A decade earlier, Bruno did the old boss another service, according to the FBI: he was involved in the South Philly execution of man spreading rumors that Sabella was cheating on his wife with a neighborhood woman.

The dead man was found facedown in the gutter, three bullets in his skull. The killers were never found, although Natale knows who pulled the trigger: his old pal DiTullio. Bruno gained a reputation as a man who treated his men fairly, affording them respect both personally and financially.

As a boy, young Ralph already knew who Bruno was: "Skinny told me, 'Ang will never do anything wrong. Never. He's that kind of a man.' It's a simple thing. When Ang would walk into a bar, everybody would stand up. Everybody."

DiTullio was just as quick to vouch for Natale with the new boss. "Skinny told him, 'Whenever I'm on vacation, in the hospital, or sick or whatever, there's only one guy who will do what you ask—fast, without talking, without anything. All you gotta do is tell him, and that's Ralph,'" Natale said.

When DiTullio filled Natale in on the Commission's endorsement of Bruno, the protégé had just one question for his mentor: "Is that what you want?"

The older man leaned over and kissed Natale, and the two raised their glasses of Scotch in a toast to Bruno—and the future.

Natale, like most in South Philly, grew up hearing about the legendary Bruno. As a kid, Ralph hung out at the corner of South Sixth Street and Manton Street. The neighborhood would buzz when the Philadelphia capo came cruising through the neighborhood with his driver at the wheel.

"Always in an old, beat-up Chevy, an old car," Natale recalled of the drive-bys. "He was affable for a mob boss. He was one of those guys, when we were thirteen, fourteen years old, he'd pass by and make the guy stop and beep the horn. Kids would yell, 'Hey, Mr. Bruno!'"

When Bruno chose an underboss, he followed the sage counsel of Gambino to the letter. Within a week, Iezzi was driving the new padrone to the Italian Market for a meeting with Phil Testa.

Testa came to Bruno's attention through one of Natale's pinpoints in time, where what a man is and what he will become are forever altered in a few unexpected minutes—often without warning. The Chicken Man, as he was known, was butchering a pair of hens for a customer when the sound of loud voices came from an adjoining shop.

Testa, the bloody butcher's knife still in hand, came to his neighbor's aid. Once inside the fish store, Testa spied local extortionist Pauly Tropea with a revolver pointed at its owner—a pal of the Sicilian-born Testa's. The Chicken Man plunged the blade into Tropea's side and simultaneously kicked the gunman's right leg out from under him.

Blood spewed like a geyser. Testa and his pal dragged Tropea's corpse outside and left him on the sidewalk. The other Sicilian business owners turned their heads in a silent message: we didn't see anything. Testa told the businessman to call the cops and report that Tropea was stabbed outside the store by a black man who fled.

Natale recalls blaming such violence on an unidentified "black guy" was almost a neighborhood tradition among the insular Italians. The local homicide cops "knew the answer before they asked the question," said Natale. "But as a matter of policy, they asked anyway."

The Black Mafia, an African-American group operating in a minority neighborhood, eventually turned the oft-repeated line on its head. When asked about murders in their sphere of influence, they developed a stock answer: "It looked like a couple of Italians did it."

Either way, the cops found collars were hard to come by.

Word soon spread along Ninth Street of Testa's bold move. Eventually, the talk made its way to Angelo Bruno. One year earlier, family capo Freddie Iezzi had touted Testa as a candidate for La Cosa Nostra. He was inducted in the usual ritual, sharing his blood finger to finger in a dark cellar on Mercy Street in South Philly.

Testa was assigned to the Bruno crew. "And so, the second life of Phil Testa began," Natale observed.

When Bruno arrived at the Italian Market seeking Testa as his number two man, it was a major event: the new don of the Philadelphia Mafia walking among his fellow Sicilians. This was their new godfather, the man they would seek out

in times of need or in want of a favor. Bruno walked pur-
posefully past the small businesses, headed for the butcher's
shop, and looked his new underboss in the eyes.

The selection didn't sit well with at least one made man,
Anthony "Tony Bananas" Caponigro, who considered the
decision a snub. Based in Newark, the mob killer showed a
loyal face to the new boss and his number two man. But an
undercurrent of anger would fester for two decades before
finally exploding.

6

One night in late February 1964, Skinny Razor sat with Natale at the bar of the Friendly Tavern and told him the eye-opening tale of the Cassius Clay–Sonny Liston fight, its rematch, and the reach of organized crime into the highest level of professional sports.

By 1964, Sonny Liston was not only the heavyweight boxing champion of the world—he was the undisputed biggest and baddest motherfucker on planet Earth, both terrifying and devastating. He never learned to read or write as a child and once recalled that "the only thing my father ever gave me was a beating." After turning pro in 1953, it was Sonny handing out the beatings as he won thirty-three of his first thirty-four bouts.

The ex-con learned to box while behind bars, coming from nothing to seize the championship belt in stunning style. He battered the preceding champion—nice guy Floyd Patterson—into submission in two one-sided bouts, much to the horror of Middle America and many ring aficionados.

The first fight, on September 25, 1962, lasted all off 126 seconds before Liston knocked the champ out.

The rematch ten months later took just seventeen seconds longer, with the same brutal result: Liston by knockout.

"The world of sport now realizes it has gotten Charles 'Sonny' Liston to keep," wrote *Los Angeles Times* sports columnist Jim Murray. "It is like finding a live bat on a string under your Christmas tree."

Liston's rise through the ranks was aided by one of Philadelphia's own: Frank "Blinky" Palermo, the notorious mob fixer of the fight game. The fighter signed on with manager Joe "Pep" Barone, who was linked with Palermo and his equally disreputable partner, New York mobster Frankie Carbo—known in mob circles as the Man in Gray, reflecting the color of his suits. His mob palette included various other shades, including work as a hit man.

"He killed Benjamin 'Bugsy' Siegel," Ralph said. "Not [his girlfriend] Virginia Hill's brother or anybody else. The mob sent Frankie Carbo. Killed him. The guy who gave him up was that little weasel Jew, Meyer Lansky—said, 'You can do what you want, he's crazy!' He gave Siegel up."

Palermo and Carbo controlled some fighters directly, and others more surreptitiously. Fights were famously fixed, as Jake LaMotta wrote in his biography, and the mob money routinely rolled in. "The Gambinos and Philadelphia owned professional boxing together," said Natale.

Carbo once boasted of exercising absolute control of the welterweight division for a full quarter century. Everyone and everything in the world of boxing operated within their orbit, as lightweight Ike Williams attested.

"See these eyes?" he once asked. "These aren't even my real eyes. Blinky robbed me blind!"

The City of Brotherly Love became the surly Liston's adopted hometown as he pounded his way to the top of the fight game. His sparring partners occasionally included Natale's driver, Frankie Vadino, Ralphy's "suit of armor"—his army of one.

"He stayed with us in Philadelphia," Natale recalled. "Blinky got him a nice apartment, this, that, got him everything. You know, he was a big heroin user. But when he was training, he'd stop and try to get ready. He was on it since he was young. A shame. Nice guy. He looked like a bear. He could fight ten guys. I mean, tremendous puncher—and he could take a punch."

Liston's next opponent was a brash young Olympic gold medalist by the name of Cassius Clay, soon to be Muhammad Ali, renowned under either name as much for his trash talk as his estimable skills inside the ring. A Liston victory over the young loudmouth was generally considered a fait accompli. "He could beat three Muhammad Alis at once in the ring—that's Sonny Liston!" was Natale's assessment.

By the time of the fight, Palermo and Carbo were behind bars after a conviction for trying to muscle in on welterweight champion Don Jordan. The duo were found guilty in 1961 of ordering a beat-down on a California promoter in their bid to seize control of Jordan's career, with Carbo warning the victim that the mob would tear out his eyeballs.

But their reach was hardly limited by their jail time, as the world was about to learn.

"There came a time when Liston was getting heavy with the heroin in between fights," recalled Natale. "Instead of withdrawing, he's using all the time now. We knew the guys who were selling the heroin, but you couldn't stop them. You bury two of them, and ten take their place—they're like cockroaches.

"So they're getting ready for this Liston fight with Ali, and they sent word from New York: 'We're gonna make the score of a lifetime.' Because you never know when he's going to OD, this guy. He's a commodity they don't want to lose. Sonny Liston, heavyweight champion! If he dies, they don't get nothing. Everything is business, so he's gotta take a dive. He's gotta dump. Whatever he does, he can't beat Ali."

On February 25, 1964, the glowering Liston stood in his corner to face the motormouth from Louisville, Kentucky. The fight was held in Miami Beach, Florida, with Clay expected to land in roughly the same spot on the canvas as Patterson—and in about the same, short amount of ring time. The betting odds reflected that sentiment.

"The opening price in Vegas was ten to one," recalled Natale. "Then it dropped to eight to one. Only the bosses knew what was going down."

Disaster nearly struck when Clay—his eyes blinded by some unidentified substance—nearly refused to come out for the fifth round. Trainer Angelo Dundee shoved his fighter back in the ring, and the bout continued as mob bosses from coast to coast exhaled deeply. Clay triumphed when Liston conceded from his corner, sitting on a stool and spitting out his mouthguard before the seventh round.

Rumors of a fix began floating immediately. The FBI investigated. Nothing was ever proven. But John DiTullio knew the truth, as told to him by Angelo Bruno.

On the night after the stunning TKO, Skinny Razor asked Natale to stick around for one of their late-night talks in the quiet confines of his bar. There, with the jukebox jazz as their sound track, he laid out the whole scenario for his protégé.

DiTullio, after telling the entire incredible tale, explained his motivation for sharing the story.

"Skinny says, 'I'm telling you this 'cause I want you to know—things can be done like this. We made the biggest score of a lifetime, legitimately, on this fight. We all took Cassius Clay,'" Natale recalled. "And throughout the country it was done. They all bet big. Not my business how much, but they made a fortune on it. All the top people, from Chicago to Milwaukee, New York, Cleveland.

"They took care of Sonny. They mighta gave him six hundred thousand dollars, seven hundred thousand dollars. He's gonna blow it all on heroin anyway, the bum."

Incredibly, the once-in-a-lifetime mob windfall repeated itself—there would be a rematch. "They started salivating again," said Natale. The immediate problem was that Liston declared that he intended to exact revenge on Clay, much to the consternation of his mob handlers.

"They told him, 'You can't win,'" Natale related. "He said, 'I'll knock him deep.' Frankie [Carbo] sent word: 'I ain't killed a man in a long time, but I'll kill you.' That was the end of that. He threw the other fight, too."

The second fight was moved to remote Lewiston, Maine, with a mere 2,434 people in attendance—the smallest crowd ever for a heavyweight title fight. The obscure rematch location was no accident.

"Who's gonna bother them there, in Lewiston, Maine?" Natale asked archly. "And he threw it twice."

Less than two minutes into round one, the once-invincible Liston collapsed to the canvas from a blow that nobody saw—Ali's infamous "phantom punch." The new champ, in an iconic photo, stood victorious over his vanquished foe, unaware of the Mafia-orchestrated backstory that came with his title belt. He was blissfully unaware of the circumstances surrounding his two not-so-stunning upsets.

"They paid him again, Liston," said Natale. "And they loaded up. They made a fortune, they really did. And Frank 'Blinky' Palermo was instrumental in the whole thing because he had the reins. It happened that way."

There was no happy ending for Liston, who was found dead in his Las Vegas home on January 5, 1971. Despite the mysterious circumstances surrounding Sonny's demise, Natale remains certain of the cause of death: "He OD'd. If the mob had killed him, I would have heard about it. He loved heroin."

7

DOING THE WORK

The tale of Sonny Liston and the multimillion-dollar haul was not the stuff of the mob's day-to-day operations. Natale moved comfortably through that world, working as Bruno's mob Mr. Fix-It in the 1960s. One day, a problem arose with a couple of porno shops/peep shows operating on Market Street. The two businesses belonged to a man from New York, the well-dressed and well-respected Robert DiBernardo.

DiB, as he was known to his friends, was a huge money-maker for the Gambino family, becoming the king of mob porn and peep shows—including part ownership of the notorious Show World Center just off Times Square. Bruno, after a call from his friend Carlo Gambino, gave DiB the go-ahead to open a peep show in Philadelphia. Both mob dons received a taste of the profits, and business was good.

Then, as Natale recalled it, a local biker gang showed up.

"They went in there and said they ran all the girl dancers and started shaking the owners down," Natale said.

"So Carlo Gambino, he's paying Ang—you're supposed to take care of these things. Gambino wants to know what's going on."

Bruno reached out to his legitimate business partner, "Long John" Martorano, who grabbed a pal and headed down to Market Street.

"You know what they tell him? 'Go fuck yourself. The girls belong to us. We don't give a fuck who sent you. We gotta get some money out of this.' They sent another guy, they told him, 'Get the fuck away from us,'" Natale remembered. "Now Ang tells Long John, 'Get the Chinaman.'"

That was Bruno's nickname for Natale. "He said, 'Your face, I couldn't tell if you were happy or unhappy or whatever,'" Natale recalled with a chuckle. "And I called him the Chief. Nobody else was allowed to do that."

Bruno's directions were simple—the bikers were making him look bad with his friend in New York. Take care of it.

Natale couldn't resist the chance to tweak the Chief. "I said, 'Didn't you already send those other guys up there?' He knew I liked to give it to him every once in a while. I always told him the same thing: 'Give me two weeks and it will be done. What do you want me to say, two days? Two weeks.' And somebody was found shot in a car, shot or whatever. The bikers, they moved out—completely."

A delighted DiB invited Natale to Little Italy for the annual Feast of San Gennaro, a mob-run street party. The Gambino capo offered to cover all expenses. Natale, never a fan of the New York families, tried unsuccessfully to stay home.

"Ang knew how I felt about these New Yorkers, they're never around for you. Plus it cost you four hundred dollars to park in New York, even then!" Natale recalled. "They all think that driving a green car is bad luck, and I drove a green Buick."

But he soon found himself in a darkened Little Italy restaurant, shaking hands with the grateful Mr. DiBernardo. They ate and drank a bit, and then DiB invited Natale for a walk through the neighborhood. It was time to put away the cannoli and talk turkey.

"He says, 'You know my principal business. Would you like to get into that? I could set you up. You don't need anything—I've got the studios, I've got everything,'" recalled Natale, who had never even been inside a peep-show booth. "I was doing so good at that time, I said I appreciated it, but I did what I did for you know who. And I'd do it again if he asked. I never mentioned [Bruno's] name in my lifetime. He says, 'If you ever change your mind, you let me know.'"

DiB later made headlines when his name surfaced in the 1984 presidential race, with allegations that he rented space from vice-presidential candidate Geraldine Ferraro's husband. Two years later, DiB was murdered on orders from Gambino family boss John Gotti.

The Philly peep-show operation was, in the grand scheme of the Mafia, small potatoes. Bruno and Gambino, it turned out, had much bigger fish to fry in Atlantic City.

8

WHERE THE SAND IS TURNIN' TO GOLD

By the 1960s, once-proud Atlantic City was reeling: The easy money was long gone, the boardwalk was seedy, the future was as bleak as a December sky over the waves crashing on the Atlantic shoreline. The truth was undeniable: the seaside resort was now little more than Bayonne with a beach.

But the city had long provided a haven for the mob, going back to the days of bootlegging and the stewardship of Enoch "Nucky" Johnson—a visionary whose exploits became fodder for the HBO show *Boardwalk Empire*. To Mafia men with the same foresight, rumors of legalized gambling in Atlantic City sounded like thousands of cash registers ringing.

Few could see the future more clearly than Carlo Gambino, the head of the nation's most powerful mob family, the New York borgata that bore his name. He presciently conjured dollar signs among the desolation.

In 1966, Bruno was called to the Ferrara Bakery and Café, a *pasticceria* in Little Italy, to discuss the future with his friend and Mafia mentor Gambino. The scent of anise and lemon floated in the air as the two men of substance and power sat amid the regulars ordering their cappuccinos and Italian pastries. The pair shared espresso and a plate of biscotti.

Two octogenarian men sitting nearby recognized Gambino. They discreetly took off their caps and lowered their eyes in recognition. Gambino offered a gracious smile in response before getting down to business.

The topic was the decrepit shorefront city under control of the Philadelphia family. Word had reached Gambino, through Wall Street–connected lawyers working for his sons Thomas and Joseph, that a quiet but steady drumbeat had started for casino gambling in Atlantic City. There was no timetable, but Gambino—though no Boy Scout—was always prepared.

The wheels were set in motion to insure the Mafia would land on the ground floor of the new casinos rising on the boardwalk. With Bruno on board, Gambino broached the idea of bringing in the Chicago family—the Outfit, as it was known, the mob birthed in blood by Al Capone. The family was experienced in the ways of unions and legalized gambling from decades entrenched in Las Vegas.

It was Gambino, not Bruno, who suggested Natale could be of service in the mob's new enterprise. Gambino spoke in a whisper, leaning forward so the conversation would remain between the two of them: "Angelo, a few years ago you had a young man meet with me at my son's office at the trucking company. I think his name was Natale. You made a comment about this young man that I put here"—pointing to his head—"for such a time as now. Am I mistaken?"

Bruno smiled at the mention of his young friend—and the encyclopedic memory of his older one. "Yes, Carlo. You don't forget too much, do you?"

Gambino broached Natale's name for a position in Local

170 of the bartenders' union, giving the mob a legitimate foothold when the new Atlantic City opened for business. Gambino said the two East Coast bosses needed to send an emissary to the Windy City, where the mighty Tony Accardo ruled and ran the mob-controlled unions. His nickname, Joe Batters, came from a penchant for applying a Louisville Slugger on the heads of those who ran afoul of his rule.

"This young man of yours," Gambino said in measured tones, "might be the one."

Bruno was immediately aware of the enormity of this discussion: three families, working together, to make a fortune from casinos that did not now exist even on some architect's drawing board. Yet he unhesitatingly jumped in with both feet.

"Ralphy has my complete trust," he answered firmly. "His loyalty shall be shared by you and me when we send him to our friends in Chicago as our man."

Gambino agreed, and so it was—over coffee, in a restaurant on Grand Street—that the mob began carving up Atlantic City before the first foundation was poured. The decision, though it would bear bitter fruit for both families in the ensuing decades, seemed a stroke of genius on this day. Gambino would handle the arrangements with Chicago.

Natale recalled how Bruno broke the news to him: "Ang told me that Gambino—he remembered me, he was a wise old man—he remembered that Ang told him, 'This guy would kill for me, without question and without causing a furor.' And Gambino said, 'Don't you think we should send him to Chicago?'

"Then we met: me, Angelo Bruno, and Carlo Gambino, before I went to Chicago. We made a pact: This is till the day we die. The three of us. And they sent word to Chicago:

It's not just Ang. It's Bruno and Gambino that I represent. Nobody ever got that part. How do they think I got there? Because I'm handsome?

"I'm not bad looking. But six feet tall, I'm not."

The promotion came with an unexpected bonus: Natale would become a made man. He had rejected the offer before, but this time it was made directly by Gambino and Bruno.

"Skinny Razor had asked me if I wanted to get made," Natale recounted. "I told him, 'You're gonna get me killed! Don't do that!' Because I really didn't like a lot of skippers in the family. I knew I would get in trouble because their word is the rule. And Skinny told me, 'Ang knows who you are, and what you are.' That was good enough for me.

"I had the best of everything because I was a part of it but I didn't have to answer to anybody. That wasn't for me— 'Oh, skipper, here I am.' You know what I'm saying? I wasn't gonna do it if they put me under somebody besides Skinny Razor, and he had a small crew."

But this time, it was the proverbial offer that Natale couldn't refuse—membership as a made man by direct invitation from his boss and the most powerful mafioso in the United States. The highly unusual ceremony, attended by just the three men, was held in a Gambino-controlled building inside Manhattan's Garment District.

"Ang and Carlo got together, and they told me, 'Don't tell anybody about this,'" Natale remembered of that day. "We pricked our fingers and put our blood together. Carlo Gambino told me, 'You belong to me now, and you belong to Ang.' Of course, I was honored."

For Natale, it was the unexpected pinnacle of his life in

organized crime: "I left there feeling like I was untouchable. I felt like I could do anything for my wife and family that I ever wanted to do. I felt almost invincible."

But the newly made man had work to do. Within weeks, Natale was winging west to meet with Ed Miller, the president of the Hotel Employees and Restaurant Employees International Union. The occasion was a convention called in the city where Accardo reigned supreme.

"Carlo Gambino always believed in acting swiftly," Natale explained. He arrived, as instructed, at the Sherman Hotel in downtown Chicago and waited in his room for a phone call. When it came, union official Phil Valli—who was tied both to Chicago and to Milwaukee boss Frank "Mr. Big" Balistrieri—was down in the lobby. Valli said he was coming upstairs. Natale hung up and waited. A soft knock came, and Natale—more out of habit than anything else—peered through the peephole. He opened the door, and Ralph Natale's future walked into the room.

The two men shook hands and exchanged pleasantries before heading downstairs to meet with Miller at the hotel bar. Natale was dressed more like an English banker than a mob killer: dark blue pinstripe suit, solid burgundy tie over a white-on-white shirt, a pair of highly polished Allen Edmonds shoes on his feet.

"You look like you're supposed to look," Valli declared after sizing up the five-foot-six Natale.

The Sherman's cocktail lounge featured a huge horseshoe-shaped bar, flanked by tables filled with conventioneers. Valli steered Natale through the crowd to the spot at the bar where Miller held court, surrounded by his own retinue of sycophants hanging on his every word. Natale approached slowly, waiting for an invitation from Miller in a show of respect for the union head. Natale would only speak once spoken to.

"Who am I to walk up when he's talking to one of the vice presidents?" Natale said of his respectful reticence. "You should never approach a man of power, or a dangerous man, quickly. I learned that young."

Miller, once a union leg-breaker, had worked his way up through the ranks to his current lofty position. As Natale hung back, Valli and Miller spoke. Valli finally gestured for Natale to join them.

"I am Ed Miller," the man declared in a whiskey rasp. "I know who you are." The introduction was followed by a smile and a firm handshake that spoke volumes to Natale about the man, who was four decades his senior. Decades later, he recalled looking into Miller's eyes: "They had seen it all. He was the real deal." Natale knew immediately he was in the presence of a kindred spirit.

Miller asked if Natale wanted a drink. "I'll have what you're drinking, Mr. Miller," he replied respectfully. "It has a great aroma."

Miller summoned the barkeep: "Dutch, give everyone fresh drinks. And give me and my young friend here a couple of Bushmills straight up, with water chasers, so we can converse intelligently." The two raised their glasses in a toast before any business began.

"I felt a comfort drinking with Miller, like I had known him forever," Natale said. "I knew that I and this old cowboy from Kansas City would talk, and everything would be as the three old men"—Gambino, Accardo, and Bruno—"would want it to be."

The next day, Natale was appointed as a special international union organizer, with powers to negotiate contracts everywhere and anywhere. The mob stars had aligned, and the future of Atlantic City—for better or worse—was a done deal for the three crime families. All they had to do now was wait. And wait they did, patiently, for a full decade.

In November 1974, the voters of New Jersey rejected a referendum to legalize gambling in the dilapidated shore resort. Two years later, by a slim measure, the vote went the other way. Atlantic City's first casino, Resorts International, opened its doors on May 26, 1978.

In the interim, Natale became head of Local 170 in the late sixties, earning a modest $18,500 a year plus another $1,500 for his work with the international. Despite the five-figure on-the-books salary, he owned a $45,000 four-bedroom home in Pennsauken, New Jersey, and a second home in Palm Springs, California. Natale also boasted a $100,000 condo that he considered an investment. His reach soon included virtually all the union locals on the East Coast.

"I liked it right away," he said of the union job. "We took that union over in New Jersey. I told them, 'Who's your lawyer? How much does he charge you? He was on a retainer of one thousand dollars a month, plus whatever he does he's charging us extra. I said, 'Gimme all the contracts. We're done with him. Now call him on the phone.' I told him, 'We can't afford you.' And then I made my own contracts up, just following what he did. What am I, a moron?"

Ralph and Lucia enjoyed the perks of his new gig. In contrast to the future Genovese family boss Vincent "the Chin" Gigante, who spent most of his life without leaving the crowded Greenwich Village streets where he was born and raised, Natale traveled far and wide on the union's dime: Miami, Belle Harbor, Florida, San Francisco, Hawaii . . .

Speaker of the House Tip O'Neill once popped in for a drink at the Palm Springs house. Natale loved the horses, and he would take Lucia to the venerable Saratoga racetrack in the summer to watch the races and the people.

"I did union work in Boston, Detroit, Milwaukee, California—anyplace I had to go and take care of business," he explained. "I was welcomed everywhere, by the bosses and capos. It was a great thing."

The Natales traveled to a Teamsters convention in Honolulu, where they checked into a nice Sheraton hotel. Natale was given a ceremonial position at the event so he could pocket a few extra bucks each day. He then headed to the host hotel, a Hilton overlooking the sparkling blue waters of the Pacific Ocean, to check in with union boss Ed Hanley as Lucia did some island shopping, Hanley was outraged that the Natales weren't staying in the Hilton.

"I said it was just too crowded, I couldn't get a room over there," Ralph said. "He told one of his stooges, call up the Sheraton, go over there and pick everything up, and bring it over here. Now."

Problem solved. Life was good, and getting better all the time.

Before long Natale had a face-to-face meeting with the nation's most powerful union boss, Teamsters president James Riddle Hoffa. The get-together was arranged by Anthony Provenzano, known to one and all as Tony Pro—and to a select few as a capo in the Genovese family. Provenzano ran the powerful Teamsters Local 560, based in Union City, New Jersey, and was part of Hoffa's inner circle.

"Tony asked me, 'Would you like to meet him?'" Natale recalled. "Just take a plane to Detroit. We'll set it up."

Hoffa and Natale became fast friends, sharing a mutual

admiration that transcended their profitable business relationship. They shared a similar view of life, a good sense of humor, and a particular bluntness in conversation.

"A man's man," Natale recalled. "He didn't have anything else besides the union. I always said he didn't drink, he didn't chase women. He was complete power—controlled all the transit, from coast to coast. I respected him so much as a man."

Once Natale reached the Motor City, he received a call with details about the time and place for their initial encounter.

"I didn't know Detroit, so they had to tell me where to go," he said. "I walked in, and he looked so good—Jimmy Hoffa, with some of his men. He was a real man, a smart man, a wise man. We shook hands, and of course I waited for him to speak first. What he said was simple: 'You wouldn't be here unless you were the man I was told you are. And I'm told you know what to do, and how to do it.'"

Natale didn't need an interpreter and replied, "I'm here for you. If you think you can't depend on me, then I shouldn't go back to Philadelphia."

His reply carried an unspoken message: "What I was saying was, 'If you can't trust me, you should kill me.' He knew what I meant. And he said, 'Okay, now you can have anything you need—credit cards, money, whatever.' From then on, I was there whenever he needed me, for whatever he needed me for."

The first order of business was a problem with a union local in Ralph's hometown.

"I always have problems in Philadelphia," Hoffa said. "Would you mind if I ask my friends here and your friend over there, if I have little problems, can I send for you and explain something to do?"

The friends involved were the Detroit mob and Bruno—
"he never mentioned names, Jimmy," Natale recalled. "I
said, 'Why not—if my friend says okay. He's my chief.' And
Jimmy depended on me, and I liked that. I never said how
much, who, why, where? He'd give me a nice envelope, and
I never got less than fifty thousand dollars—and that was a
lot of money at that time."

Things went on from there: "We laughed and we talked.
He told me, 'Anything you want, you feel free to come
straight to me. And if there's something really important, I'll
come to see you in New Jersey.' I mentioned the names of a
few of my 'good friends,' and he told me, 'I already called
them. You have the recommendation of Tony Pro.'"

Natale recalled one of his first assignments from Hoffa:
"Somebody had a problem in the brewery down in Philadelphia, Schmidt's. They were looking to buy this and that
there, and Ang of course said, 'Ralphy, handle this. Do what
you have to do over there.'"

Natale did as he was told and earned Hoffa's enduring
respect. Without going into too much detail, Natale recalled
taking a phone call directly from the union boss to handle
another bit of business: "He said, 'Come and see me. I have
a little problem, and maybe we can fix it.' I was on a plane to
Detroit within the hour. In a couple of weeks, problem solved.
He took care of me handsomely—and whenever he called,
I answered."

According to Natale, Hoffa had a unique relationship
with the Mafia families from coast to coast. "He was connected with the mob in every city, but they never owned
him," Natale said with admiration. "They couldn't tell him
what to do. They didn't own him."

Natale's involvement with Local 170 actually predated his

role in Atlantic City and his work for Hoffa. In the late fifties, a housing boom in South Jersey produced a sudden influx of new entrepreneurs eager to serve the growing population with restaurants and nightclubs. The venerable Latin Casino, the Philly stop for such stars as Frank Sinatra and Dean Martin, pulled up stakes on Walnut Street in the city and headed to Route 70 in Cherry Hill.

The change in demographics would, as so many things did, offer the Philadelphia underworld a sparkling new revenue stream. The employees at these new businesses became members of Local 170, then under the command of Joe Siedman and Sam Rifkin—two men with "friends" of their own.

Unlike most unions, this one appeared more concerned with the business owners than the rank and file, cutting a series of sweetheart deals that benefited the businesses and the two local leaders more than the membership.

Unfortunately for Siedman and Rifkin, workers moving from the Philly union to Local 170 soon became acutely aware of the difference in the way things operated on the Jersey side of the Walt Whitman Bridge. The money was less, and the health benefits were meager. A group of dissidents grew, headed by a pair of waiters from Philly and a Cherry Hill bartender. They were soon appearing at every union meeting and nominating their own slate of candidates to run the show.

A loss would mean the end of the cash-stuffed envelopes for Siedman and Rifkin that came once a month from the local businesses and the Cadillac Linen Co.—two groups brought together by the union. Both of those groups belonged to Philly's "Jew Mob"—headed by a pair of contract killers once aligned with Louis "Lepke" Buchalter's infamous

Murder, Inc. A change in leadership would hit the pair directly in their wallets, as the dissidents soon learned. The challengers decided they would not back down, but instead recruited some muscle of their own: two ex–amateur boxers who once worked as strong-arm organizers for the Teamsters.

Richard "Bucky" Baldino and Joe McGreal were summoned by the dissident leaders. Baldino, a man of fierce reputation, suggested they needed a third man: his old boyhood friend Ralph Natale, currently aligned with the DiTullio crew of the Bruno family. Baldino reasoned, quite accurately, that Natale was the man they needed if their takeover bid should run afoul of the Jew Mob.

The challengers triumphed overwhelmingly in the election. Siedman and Rifkin were out. And the new leadership was suddenly in—too deep, as it turned out. Natale recalled election night as "a gush of fresh blood in the ocean, with a couple of great white sharks circling nearby."

The sharks were McGreal and Natale. But before they would eat, Natale had to make things right with Philly's two top Jewish gangsters, men of great repute and a pair of stone killers.

A luncheon get-together was arranged, with Natale heading to the rival mob's home turf.

The two hulking men at the front door of Rose Linchik's restaurant greeted Natale and his driver by name, though neither recognized the pair. The restaurant was closed for the day, but opened specifically to welcome the Italian visitors entering off the narrow stretch of Quince Street.

Driver Frankie Vadino was ordered to wait downstairs while Natale headed to the private dining room where Willie Weisberg and Cappy Hoffman awaited. The two were the heads of the local Jew Mob, legends of the Philadelphia underworld, and onetime contract killers for Murder, Inc.

Natale was well aware that through the years the two had hosted many last meals in this very spot for unwitting victims. Before heading upstairs, Natale spoke to his driver: "Frankie, if you hear shots from upstairs, open up on whoever you're with and screw. Don't worry about me. I'll already be dead."

The driver nodded, and Natale started up the staircase. He was at peace with whatever happened: "If that's what is supposed to be, it's too late now to be scared." Thoughts of prior lunches when Angelo Bruno and he summoned a poor unfortunate to a meal that ended in murder drifted through his mind.

When Natale reached the landing upstairs, two men who looked more like tailors than hit men awaited. Weisberg greeted him with a question: "Are you armed?"

Ralphy knew better than to lie. He never blinked or hesitated. "Yes, I am."

"Ralphy," declared a smiling Hoffman, "I would do the same thing coming to lunch with us two old gangsters."

With the mood lightened, owner Rose Linchik headed to their table to take a lunch order. "They say the chicken soup here is to die for," deadpanned Natale as the tension in the room dissipated. Weisman quickly got down to business, noting that previous union heads Siedman and Rifkin were generous business partners through the years.

The conversation was interrupted by the arrival of the soup, accompanied by a basket of dark bread and a slab of unsalted butter. "Eat and be well," the owner advised Natale, who was by now fairly certain that he would do both.

Weisman grabbed a piece of the bread, smeared it with

butter, and said, "You eat, Ralphy. And I'll talk. Angelo told me that he said only this to you, that we were his friends long before any unions."

"That's true," Natale responded evenly.

Weisman continued speaking as Natale kept eating. Finally, with the chicken soup gone, the younger man felt that he could resolve the issues at hand:

"What you and Cappy has stays the same, and if we could get more for you, I'll make sure it will get done. My respect for you and Cappy doesn't come down to dollars and cents. The both of you were gangsters when I was peeing off curbs. Nothing changes."

All three men stood, exchanging smiles before shaking hands. They came from different eras, Natale reflected, but they were men cut from the same cloth. The Philadelphia family was in. And one day, the union would fall under Ralph's control.

9

AN IRISH WAKE

The 1970s arrived with a new problem for Natale, and his name was George Feeney. He was a tough guy, a hard-drinking Irishman who liked to run his mouth after a few belts, with a tendency to say things that soon proved hazardous to his health.

Feeney was an ex-con affiliated with local union boss Joe McGreal. Natale soon caught wind of Feeney's intemperate comments, particularly regarding Natale's friend and boss.

"It was starting to get around the city: 'That man downtown, he ain't nothing,'" Natale said. "Meaning Angelo Bruno. Some good people heard that. He coulda got killed just for that. People told me they heard what he said. I said, 'This motherfucker. I'll kill him today. He ain't nothing.'"

Firsthand confirmation came from McGreal, who reported that Feeney was out of control and talking out of school. McGreal finally called Natale one morning at 7:30 a.m. for a sit-down at the Half-Hour Club, a bar owned by McGreal's brother. Natale appeared amid the morning boozers with a solution.

"I said, 'Well, call him now. Tell him you wanna talk to him. And when he shows up, I'll splatter his fucking brains,'" Natale matter-of-factly recalled.

McGreal was stunned: "Ralphy, it's broad daylight! Everybody's gonna see!"

A plan was hatched: They would meet up with Feeney that Sunday at Billy Duke's, a club on Route 73 in Jersey. From there, all three would go down to a bar in Swampoodle— the Irish section of Philadelphia. McGreal implored Natale not to whack Feeney in the tavern.

"I said, 'Do you think I'm crazy?'" Natale remembered. "And McGreal said, 'Don't make me answer that, Ralphy!'"

The plan was put into motion—although Feeney initially blanched at going into the city from Billy Duke's. But Ralph proved persuasive, approaching Feeney in the men's room:

"I said, 'Listen, I don't want to shoot you, but I will fucking shoot you. Your friend and my friend Joey, we have a problem, and I can't have that. Let's go where we're safe. Let's go down to the Irish club.' He looked at me and said, 'Okay, I'm gonna come.'"

It was the next-to-last bad decision of George Feeney's life.

The bar was jammed and the jukebox blaring on the Sunday night when Natale arrived. He greeted the bartender, an ex-pug who once fought in Madison Square Garden. Connected with Mc Greal and Feeney, Natale suggested the three men go upstairs to the bar's office and talk. Ralph went into the second-floor bathroom and overheard the irate McGreal trying to talk some sense into his pal.

McGreal pulled a gun on Feeney, who was sitting in a chair, and started shouting: "I told you to shut your mouth!"

Then Feeney made his final faux pas. "Fuck him!" he

yelled about Natale. "And fuck the old man down there! We should kill them both!"

"I hear this as I'm coming out of the bathroom," said Natale. "I was furious. I grabbed the gun out of McGreal's hand. I put three in Feeney's face—boom, boom, boom! Right in his fucking dome. Done. Then I told McGreal, 'Get this piece of shit out of here.'"

Another union official entered the room, with Feeney's blood and brains now splattered on the floor, and nearly vomited. Problem solved.

10

When DiTullio died of a heart attack in the early seventies, Bruno summoned Natale for a one-on-one sit-down. Once they were done, Natale stepped into the shoes of the very man who'd taught him everything about the Mafia. He was honored and humbled as he exited the meeting.

"Ang said, 'You know, your friend and my dear friend is gone, but he's not gone.' I said, 'You're right, 'cause I still feel him.' And he said, 'That's not really what I meant. Because he's sitting right next to me. It's you.'

"That was all he had to say."

Natale, already a true believer, became unquestionably loyal to Bruno—eager to handle any tasks of any kind as requested by the boss. But their relationship transcended mere business. On Thursday nights, when Bruno and his wife had a weekly dinner date, he would sometimes invite the Natales along. One night, the two men were discussing how others in the crime family were jealous of their friendship.

"You're gonna face this," Bruno told him. "That's what's happening with all these other people around you."

Natale, to keep their wives from overhearing, said softly, "I don't give a fuck what they say or what they care about me. I care about you."

Looking back, Natale is sure the boss already knew what was coming before Natale said a single word: "He saw it. I didn't kiss his ass. He knew what I meant. Ang was the man I wanted to be, in my life."

Natale would get there, but the path was filled with twists and turns too treacherous to contemplate. One of the biggest came in the form of Charlie Allen, the bastard nephew of legendary gangster Blinky Palermo. Blinky's brother knocked up a local Philly girl, but couldn't pass along his name—so young Charlie took his mother's instead, even as he hung around with his father's mob cohorts.

"He was half-nuts, even as a kid," said Natale. "Hurting cats and dogs. A real screwball."

Allen, while doing federal time in Lewisburg, Pennsylvania, landed the position of bodyguard for imprisoned Teamsters boss Jimmy Hoffa. Doing time in the same penitentiary was Ralphy's old union pal McGreal, who became friendly with a Gambino family made man by the name of John Gotti. The two shared a love for conversation, often about things better off left unsaid. The penitentiary gave the two plenty of time to chat.

Years later, Gotti—by then the head of the Gambinos—died in prison after running his mouth about mob business and mob murders as FBI agents listened via wiretaps installed inside his Little Italy headquarters.

But for now, the future Dapper Don wore only a prison jumpsuit as he did time for stealing cargo from John F. Kennedy International Airport near his Queens home.

The jailhouse topic of conversation between Gotti and

McGreal was about something two hours south of the Big Apple: Atlantic City. The mouthy McGreal was the head of Local 170 of the Hotel Employees and Restaurant Employees International Union. Its ranks were certain to swell with the influx of business in the seaside resort—and the Philadelphia family had already made its intentions quite clear about grabbing control of the local union.

"Joe McGreal, he started bragging: 'I got a union,'" Natale said. "And John Gotti's another guy—'bum bum bum, I got this and I'm gonna be that.' You could bet your life on it, they're gonna get together. And they started talking about Atlantic City, because everybody thought Atlantic City would become the Vegas of the East. When Gotti hears this about the union, he doesn't know that Carlo Gambino and Angelo Bruno had joined together—it was none of his business."

Gotti, who knew enough not to get in the middle of such things, sent word to his underboss Aniello "Mr. Neil" Dellacroce about the union guy willing to throw in with the Gambinos if Atlantic City opened up. Dellacroce had a reputation as an old-school guy who took no bullshit from anyone. And he brought the news directly to his boss, Gambino.

Dellacroce was "a real man—when he was told something, he did it," recalled Natale. "'Cause if you question a boss, especially Carlo Gambino, the next morning you will not draw a breath. Gotti did his job, he sent it back to Dellacroce. And he told Gambino."

Gambino reached out to Bruno, who assured New York that he was putting Natale on the problem. Ralphy knew this talk was jeopardizing the deal reached by Gambino, Accardo, and Bruno, but he still hoped—somewhat uncharacteristically—to take care of things without any bloodshed.

"I did everything possible not to be forced to kill Mc-Greal when he was released from prison," Natale recalled. He traveled from Philadelphia to the Pennsylvania penitentiary for a jailhouse sit-down with McGreal to explain the facts of life.

"He was told in no uncertain terms that the union now belonged to La Cosa Nostra, and when he came home, he would be compensated," Natale remembered. During the prison visit, Natale assured McGreal that his cooperation would come with a golden parachute: a down payment on a beautiful home in the Jersey suburbs. A lucrative contract with Schmidt's Brewery in Philadelphia. And a brand-new Cadillac.

"That's what I got him," Natale says. "But he kept talking. I told him, 'You're making me look bad because it goes straight upstairs to Dellacroce and Gambino.' Ang was like, 'What did you do? Did you pick the wrong guy for this? This is a big deal with the gambling, with this, with that.'"

Then mouthy McGreal dropped another bombshell behind bars—this one courtesy of Charlie Allen. McGreal had pulled him aside with an offer: Kill Natale and collect your share of the pot of gold soon to arrive in Atlantic City. Allen, who generally would kill anybody for $5,000, considered his options and Ralphy's reputation. He ratted McGreal out to the mob.

"He thought, 'Ralphy's already there, Angelo loves him. I gotta be crazy,'" said Natale. He never forgot the words uttered from McGreal to Allen once they reached Philadelphia: "Don't rush it. Get it right, because Ralphy—you gotta be careful with him."

Once out of Lewisburg, Allen made a beeline to his uncle, Blinky Palermo, who unhesitatingly informed Bruno of the nascent scheme. Palermo then shared the tale with Natale as the two men sat at Ralphy's table in the main dining room at the Garden State Race Track, overlooking the finish line. Allen was looking for a reward, a pat on the back from Bruno for his information. If Palermo had told Natale first, the reception would have been far different.

Ralphy didn't trust Allen, regardless of his blood ties to his pal. His preference was to put a bullet between Charlie's eyes and let the chips fall. But before he could do anything, Natale was summoned from the racetrack to meet with Bruno. Natale called his driver, Frankie Vadino, and said he would be waiting outside the clubhouse entrance.

The call from Bruno came with a message: don't stop anywhere on the way. The boss knew how his old friend Natale would react if he ran into Allen—deliberately or not. Natale paid his tab at the track and went out to meet Vadino, climbing into the shotgun seat before they pulled away.

Natale was pissed off at Palermo for going to the boss, and the news sent his mind racing and his blood boiling. This was the kind of information that he wanted to hear first. "I was angry when I heard Allen was involved," Natale said. "After all, it was about killing me. Don't I have a right to be angry?"

There was one immediate concern: What if Allen had decided to gun Natale down instead of going to Blinky? The thought just ate at Natale as Vadino steered the Buick Electra toward the Walt Whitman Bridge and South Philly.

"Just suppose Charlie Allen came over to the track on the pretense of saying hello after doing ten years, but had something else in mind," Natale said years later. "Like putting two holes in my head while I was welcoming him home."

The two men rode in silence until Natale told Vadino to get off at Broad Street and head to Bruno's home.

Vadino finally broke the uncomfortable quiet. "What's up?" wondered the typically taciturn driver.

"That Irishman," Ralph responded tersely, "has decided to be more than he was ever intended to be."

Natale then laid the whole thing out to his driver: Palermo had gone to Bruno first to save his nephew's life. He knew that Natale would unquestionably whack Allen, as both an act of self-preservation and a message to McGreal and anybody else that Natale was not to be fucked with.

"What are we gonna do?" asked Vadino.

"I'll tell you what we're gonna do," Natale snapped. "We're gonna turn right on Snyder Avenue and go see the chief." The tone indicated this was the last answer coming from Natale for the rest of the ride. The two men drove on, accompanied only by the sounds of the car's engine and its four spinning wheels. Vadino parked out front and waited outside as Natale knocked gently on the boss's front door.

Bruno was blunt when Natale came inside: "It's about the Irishman in your neighborhood. He's trying to be something he ain't." It wasn't the first time that the two had had this conversation, and Natale assured the boss that everything was under control.

"Don't worry about it," said Natale. "I'm gonna go up and see him."

Bruno was just as blunt about Allen: Not only would he live, but he would join Natale's crew over in New Jersey. And so it was said, as Natale often observed, and so it was done.

"Make sure he makes a living," Bruno counseled. "Because he gave up McGreal about killing you, and maybe killing me, too."

"Angelo Bruno inadvertently caused the downfall of me and my crew and opened the doors for the treachery in Tony Bananas' heart," Natale said decades later. Ralph found a place for Allen with his crew, handling chores from arson for hire to extorting local businesses to truck hijackings.

Natale made his second trip to Lewisburg in six months, meeting again in the visitors' room with McGreal. The sit-down was brief, with McGreal implausibly insisting that he had said nothing to anyone about the union situation—much less a word to anybody from the New York families. He thanked Natale for the help coming his way once he returned to the streets. The two men shook hands, with Natale looking into McGreal's eyes and seeing nothing.

On the ride home, Natale thought of an old adage: "If a man does not listen to the first note of the song, he will never listen to the rest."

The trip that Natale never took was the one he most wanted to make: a visit with Charlie Allen.

"I woulda went to see him," Natale said. "I woulda killed him and anybody he's with. I don't care if he's in his mother's house—she's gonna go, too. I'm gonna kill him. And now I'm looking at Blinky. What am I gonna do?"

The loyal soldier and friend, instead of following his instinct, did nothing. He even gave Allen a second pass after the mob underling griped that his partner in a series of hijackings deserved a bigger cut of the pie.

"I said, 'More? For what?'" Natale recalled. "I looked at him. You know what was in my heart? I'm gonna kill him. I told him, 'Why don't you meet me tomorrow, at the Holiday Inn, in the back? Seven o'clock in the morning, we could talk.'

"That morning, I got in the car. In the five-minute ride,

I said, 'What a mistake I made.' Truth on my children. I see his car back there, and I said, 'I can't kill this guy. I gotta give him a chance.' So this is my life, and I didn't kill him."

Charlie Allen, like a bad penny, would resurface to remind Natale of his error in judgment. But Natale now had something more pressing on his plate: the murder of Mc-Greal, as directed by his boss.

"Joe McGreal's fate was sealed, as sure as the spring follows winter," Natale decided. "I said to myself, 'Joe McGreal is a dead man.'"

Three years after McGreal watched in disbelief as Natale whacked Feeney, it was his turn—on Christmas night 1973, on direct orders from Angelo Bruno. After Natale left his family around the television, he went to meet with his unsuspecting target. McGreal—godfather to one of Natale's daughters—never realized the end was near until they pulled into the darkened parking lot outside a shuttered restaurant.

During the ride to meet with McGreal, Natale reflected on the past. McGreal's cause of death, in Natale's mind, was putting his trust in a weasel such as Allen to keep his mouth shut. McGreal's destiny was now controlled by the person sitting in the backseat of a car, and his name was Ralph Natale.

"*Boom boom boom!*" Natale recalled. "Three shots in the same hole."

The timing of the killing particularly bothered Natale, who was typically immune to such thoughts. He even considered calling the whole thing off. But in the end, he pulled the trigger and pumped three hollow-point bullets into McGreal's head.

"When you take a man's tomorrows, there's more than just saying it," he reflected years later. "More, more. No matter how cold-blooded, coldhearted. Could there be a reason why? Not that there's a good reason to take anybody's tomorrows. But sometimes, it has to be done."

Joe McGreal was gone before the Christmas lights of South Philly came down.

The local TV news blared news of the mob hit throughout the next day. Natale knew that Bruno would be pleased, and his Atlantic City partners placated: the boss had picked the right man to protect their future interests.

A young Philly Turk once told Natale that his handiwork with a gun was greatly admired among the local mob cognoscenti. Wayne Grande, who later emerged as one of the most treacherous and untrustworthy mobsters in Philly's long and twisted history, recalled his dad providing a glowing review of Natale the shooter.

"He said, 'You know, Ralphy, when I was a kid—boy, how things get around,'" Natale said. "'My father, when Joe McGreal was found in the car dead, the next day my father said, "That was Ralphy."' And that was the truth."

Natale made his share of enemies—with the keen eyes of his wife, Lucia, sparing him from one hit attempt by a vengeful pal of McGreal in the midseventies.

Natale was hanging out at the Holiday Inn bar opposite the Garden State Race Track, waiting for Lucia to meet him for dinner. Their son dropped her off, and she came inside to see her husband holding court with his crew. Outside, Rick Conte sat stewing behind the wheel of his car, the murder of Ralph Natale occupying his every thought.

"All the guys stood up—'Lucia, sit here.' She said, 'Ralphy, before I sit down, can I speak to you?' I knew something was up," Natale remembered. "We walk into the lobby. She says, 'That guy, Rick, he's out in the parking lot.

He's in his car, and when he saw me, he sort of bent his head down.'

"I said to myself, 'Oh, this motherfucker—he was a pretty good boxer and a good friend of Joe McGreal. He was going around, drinking and talking: 'I'm gonna do this. I'm gonna do that. I'm gonna get even.'"

Natale assured his wife it was nothing and told her to sit down and have a drink. Then he asked his bartender pal Franny McDonnel if a certain shipment of wine had arrived.

"He knew what I meant," Ralph recalled. "I go back in where the wine is, and I told him, 'Get your .38 and come around from the back. That punk's out there. He wants to get even? I'm gonna let him try.' This is five thirty at night. The last race is over. I said, 'I'm gonna kill this motherfucker right now, in broad daylight.' I don't care.

"But he saw Franny, and then he knew I was coming. He pulled away."

Natale summoned his deadliest associates, Mike Marrone and Ronnie Turchi, and began scouring the local mob hangouts for the would-be shooter—only to come up empty. But Natale was not one to forget even the smallest of slights, much less an aborted attempt to put two bullets into his head. When their paths unexpectedly crossed a year later, every detail came flooding back.

"Ang had sent word to meet him at one p.m. at Freddie Iezzi's bar," Natale recalled. "I brought along Mike Marrone because in those days you never knew if your number was coming up, you know? There's a group of men sitting in the back of the bar with Ang and Phil Testa. Then I knew everything was all right. Ang just liked having me around."

The party included Russell Bufalino, who ran the mob's operations in northeast Pennsylvania. Natale greeted the boss with a handshake and a kiss on the cheek—a violation of Bruno's usual rules, but one that was ignored among this small group of important mafiosi.

The other guests, to Natale's disbelief, included Conte—now working for Bufalino. Ralph, though outwardly calm, felt the surge of a murderous payback rise in his suddenly boiling blood, enough that Bruno could see the signs of anger in Natale. The underling said nothing to anyone as the two bosses conducted business and watched silently as Conte left with Bufalino. Natale remained quiet even as Bruno asked him for a ride to lawyer Jacob Kossman's office. Bruno sat up front, and underboss Testa took the backseat.

The uncomfortable ten-minute quiet was finally broken by the boss. "Why did you look so aggressive when you were introduced to that young guy? What was the problem?"

The enraged Natale, throwing mob protocol to the wind, spoke the brutal truth about his feelings toward a fellow mobster from another family: "I said something that I don't think anybody ever said to any boss at any time—'The next time I see that guy, I'm gonna kill him. I don't give a fuck.'" Looking in the rearview mirror, Natale saw a small grin flash across the face of the typically dour Testa—"the first time I ever saw him smile."

Bruno was stunned by the declaration: "You're gonna give me a heart attack." But Natale recounted the racetrack tale and Conte's boozy threats in the barrooms of South Philly. When Bruno heard the details, he offered to handle the killing personally.

Natale became even angrier at the mere suggestion. "You know what I told him? 'If you do that for me, you'll lose me for the rest of my life. You can't take care of my personal business.' He's got a little smile on his face, and he said, 'Okay, just drop me off. Tomorrow morning, just make sure you come over and have coffee.'"

Natale explained his reasoning at the breakfast get-together: "Ang, I love you, but nobody's catching me with my pants on the ground. 'Cause if you take care of it, that means I'm not the man you think I am. Is that what you want him to think?"

The postscript: Natale never laid eyes on Conte again, probably the best thing for both parties. "I never found that bastard," he said ruefully.

With Natale and his growing family in the Jersey suburbs, he landed a legitimate gig tending bar once again—this time at the Rickshaw Inn, a popular spot opposite the racetrack in Cherry Hill. The place doubled as Natale's base of illegal operations.

"I wanted to make some extra money, and I enjoyed it," he said of his decision to get back behind the stick. "The owners thought I could keep a lot of trash out of there. What a magnificent place! I would meet different people there. You knew who you could trust. And it was five minutes from my house."

11

When the call came, Ralph Natale reflected on exactly how long it had been since he'd laid eyes on Jimmy Hoffa. Their final meeting was tinged with melancholy rather than the bravura of their initial get-together—a sad coda to a close friendship. Hoffa was reaching out after a run of hard luck and hard times.

For more than four years, Hoffa ran the powerful International Brotherhood of Teamsters from behind bars in Lewisburg, Pennsylvania, with his handpicked general vice president, Frank Fitzsimmons, representing the boss on the outside. Hoffa, after a brutal and bruising legal war with the government, went to jail in 1967 after convictions for conspiracy and misusing the union's pension funds.

Hoffa cut a 1971 deal for his freedom, but it came with a price: the veteran labor organizer agreed to resign his post atop the Teamsters and never again serve as a union official. Hoffa was promised, before heading to prison, that his successor Fitzsimmons could resign and surrender the union once Hoffa was back on the streets.

But things had changed in his absence, and Fitzsimmons—with the backing of some prominent mob leaders—wasn't going anywhere. Hoffa was undeterred and began angling to regain control of his union and its top spot.

"Fitzsimmons went to see (Genovese family boss) Fat Tony Salerno, who told him, 'Don't worry about him. Jimmy Hoffa will be talked to, and this will be straightened out,'" said Natale. "Of course, nobody kept their word."

The possibility of Hoffa's running for the union's top spot in 1976 soon emerged as his likeliest road to Teamsters redemption. Hoffa, behind the scenes, contacted some of his old friends to see if such a move was plausible—a clandestine tour to see who was willing to back his play.

Natale was hardly surprised by this bold move: "They couldn't change Jimmy. They could tell him what to do, but they couldn't change his manhood. He was a great union leader. And he had some balls. I heard he was gonna do this or that."

The final meeting of Natale and Hoffa took place in the Rickshaw Inn, a restaurant with a gold-flecked roof and a huge half-a-horseshoe-shaped bar opposite the Cherry Hill racetrack. A few days earlier, Natale was at the offices of Local 170 when the phone rang. It was John Greeley, head of the South Jersey Local 676 and one of area's most influential labor leaders.

"Calls me out of the clear blue sky," said Natale. "John says, 'That guy's in town. He wants to see you.' I knew what he means. And I said, 'Oh, yeah? Okay.'"

Natale, unsure what to expect, arrived for the 1:00 p.m. get-together with two killers from his crew, Turchi and Marrone—the latter a truly terrifying figure who once attended a wedding reception with a hatchet tucked in the small of his back. "Just in case," he explained.

Natale figured he was better safe than eternally sorry. "I never knew when people called me what's gonna happen," he said. " 'Cause in those days, everything was *comme ci, comme ça*—I might have some crazy people wanna take a shot at me. I'm gonna go down blazing. I ain't gonna walk into something.

"In our life, you're only killed by your friends—or people pretending to be your friends. That's our life."

His fears were unfounded. And unlike their previous meeting in Detroit, when the union world belonged to an all-powerful Hoffa and the future appeared limitless, a feeling of impending doom lingered this time.

"Anyway, I went and it was just terrible," Natale recounted. "It's about one in the afternoon, it's dark in the lounge. At the far end of the horseshoe, there's Jimmy and John Greeley. Jimmy comes up and shakes my hand. We hugged like men."

The old friends exchanged pleasantries, and before long Greeley excused himself, leaving Hoffa and Natale to discuss the business at hand: the reincarnation of James Riddle Hoffa.

Hoffa spoke first: "I heard you've been busy." Natale smiled, and then Hoffa got down to business: "I guess you know why I'm here."

"I said, 'I hear a lot of things through the grapevine.' I'd heard different people telling me about it, people that meant something.

"He said, 'Ralph, I'm gonna need some help in Jersey. John Greeley already said he was with me, if I run.' And John would. He was that kind of man. Jimmy said, 'The next convention, I'm gonna take the thing back by acclaim and I need your help. Would you help me like you always helped me?' "

Natale looked directly at the powerful union leader, a look that expressed both his admiration and the dilemma he was now facing. Finally he spoke: "Jimmy, you know who was I with since I was a boy—before I was a boy. When I was in my mother's womb, my father was with them, and I'm with them. So let me tell you one thing first: 'A man cannot serve two kings.'"

Hoffa offered a wry grin before responding, "Ralphy, I knew you were going to say that." Unmentioned was the name of Angelo Bruno, who would make the ultimate decision on Philly's support of Hoffa.

Natale then offered a biblical reference to his boss: "Listen, if he—like Pontius Pilate—washes his hands of it, says he's not involved in all this stuff against you, I'm gonna help you in a minute. I know Fitzsimmons broke his word to you, I was told by a hundred people."

Hoffa was expecting the answer, and he knew Ralph's response meant support from the Philadelphia faction was a pipe dream. He looked right back at Natale: "I knew you would say that. And I respect that. But I wish you said, 'If he looks the other way, I'll help you and do whatever you need.'"

The mood turned darker than the dim bar lights as the two old friends sat in silence, their brief conversation signaling with a black future for Hoffa. The implications were not lost on Natale, either.

"He already knew the answer, but he had to ask me," Natale said. "When he said he understood, I felt like I was at his funeral. I could smell the dirt of the grave on him. That's how I felt, right then and there in that room. I hadn't felt, up to that time, so bad in all my life, until I looked at him. I'm pretty coldhearted about these things, but my heart went out to him.

"He was dead. He was a dead man talking to me. I said, 'Jim, are you sure?'

"And he said, 'I have to do this. It's the only thing I have.' I looked at this man, who could get killed for doing what he thought was right. And he was right—he was ten times the man that Fitzsimmons was."

Natale awoke the next morning and drove directly to Bruno's house to speak with the boss about the Hoffa situation. Bruno's wife, Sue, answered his knock, and invited Ralph in for a cup of coffee and a few minutes of her husband's time. When Bruno appeared, Natale recounted his meeting at the Rickshaw.

The boss's response was hard and fast: "You know I love Jimmy. But there's no reason for him to do this. It's wrong. Even if he calls you and says it's an emergency, stay away. That man up in Jersey [Tony Provenzano] is going to take care of this. Please, don't forget what I said."

Natale, as usual, kept his mouth shut and remembered every word. The boss's edict was final, a Philadelphia epitaph for Hoffa's reign. "And I thought, 'Oh my God.' It wasn't long after that he disappeared," Natale recalled.

He never saw or spoke to Jimmy Hoffa again. The mighty labor boss disappeared on July 30, 1975.

"I couldn't get over it for weeks. I felt terrible—oh, I felt bad," Natale recalled. "And for me—I seen a lot of things, I done a lot of things—it bothered me. I respected him so much as a man."

In an odd quirk, law enforcement summoned Natale as they investigated Hoffa's death, asking about their afternoon at the Rickshaw. The mob killer was insulted at the insinuation that he was involved: "I said, 'Don't even ask that. I would never do that. You know my MO—not with friends.'"

12

Carlo Gambino died on October 15, 1976, without ever seeing his vision for Atlantic City come to fruition or fortune. The old don, before his passing, had turned control of his eponymous family to his brother-in-law Paul Castellano.

The move made sense to Gambino, whose sons were entrenched in Manhattan's Garment District. His mob family was considered the strongest and wealthiest on the East Coast, if not the nation.

To Ralphy, it was a choice fraught with disaster. The selection was driven by Gambino's greed, keeping everything that he had created in control of his own family, and not his "family." His personal fortune would be protected, and he believed Castellano would rule using the template of Gambino's reign as a guide going forward.

But many in the Gambino rank and file supported the elevation of respected underboss Aniello Dellacroce, creating a schism among the mighty family. The man known as Mr. Neil also had the respect of leaders atop the other four families of the Big Apple.

"A monumental error in judgment that was to sound the death knell for the family," Natale observed decades down the road. "He badly misjudged his capos' reactions, and those of the soldiers on the street."

The choice reminded Natale of an old Sicilian proverb: "For without the hammer, the nails would still stand upright." Castellano was not strong enough to drive the family nails.

The decision echoed on the streets in Philadelphia, too, where Bruno's alliance with the late don had long provided him with an unassailable ally—an organized crime ace in the hole. Looking back, Natale sees Castellano's rise as the beginning of everybody else's fall.

"It was the biggest mistake Gambino would ever make in his life," said Natale. "Paul thought everything was calm in his family. But greed caused all the problems, in his own family and everywhere else. Paul was a legitimate guy, too—he ran a successful company, Blue Ribbon Meats. His two sons were legitimate guys, everything would be in place.

"It doesn't work that way. He didn't know what was in these other guys' minds. He didn't read 'em right. To run a Mafia family, you gotta be the top mafioso."

Such concerns were not on the table when Castellano and Bruno—two dons doomed to die before their time—met in the hours after New Jersey voters gave their stamp of approval to casino gambling on November 2, 1976. The late-night supper at Valentine's in Cherry Hill was a time to celebrate a bright future for their two families, to toast the absolute power of La Cosa Nostra.

As the new Gambino boss, Castellano was there to assure that the decade-old deal between the families was still intact.

"Paulie, great things happen when you have patience," Bruno assured him. The Las Vegas of the East was indeed now theirs—along with the family in Chicago—the Docile Don assured his dinner companion. Castellano, trying to mask his euphoria, reached across the table to touch Bruno's hand in a show of respect.

Big Paulie recalled the words that Gambino had shared from his sickbed: Angelo Bruno was a trusted partner and an unshakable friend. His word was his bond.

Castellano told Bruno those feelings were mutual. "Angelo, I will handle everything on my end by myself, with Chicago and the Commission. And I will make sure Ralphy receives all the support needed to finish this move."

Not even a threat delivered months later by New Jersey governor Brendan Byrne could dampen the exuberance. "Keep your filthy hands out of Atlantic City," Byrne warned the mob, already too late, in June 1977. "Keep the hell out of our state."

The mob's vision for the seedy city with its no-account cast of characters was becoming a reality. Best of all for Castellano, New York City's four other families—the Genovese, Colombo, Lucchese, and Bonanno borgatas—were on the outside looking in. The combined firepower of Philadelphia and the Gambinos would keep poachers from thinking twice about wetting their beaks.

On the same celebratory night, in a bar two hours north off the New Jersey Turnpike, the first seeds of treachery were taking root despite the triumph at the polls. "Tony Bananas" Caponigro watched the election returns at his bar Down Neck in Newark, a martini sitting in front of him on the mahogany bartop. Alongside sat his brother-in-law, the made man Freddie Salerno. Both were with the Philadelphia family, and Caponigro was Bruno's consigliere—a trusted adviser.

The vote to approve casino gambling stirred only anger and bitterness in the mob veteran Caponigro. For the first time in decades, control of Atlantic City would actually lead to a cash windfall for the Philadelphia family. And now they would share their good fortune with the Gambinos of New York? The thought ate at Caponigro, who nursed a long-standing grudge against Carlo Gambino.

Way back when, the ruling Commission declared Newark an "open city"—free for any of the five families or the Philadelphia faction to conduct business. The ruling rankled Caponigro, the lookout man for the two shooters in the October 23, 1935, murder of bootlegger Dutch Schultz at the Palace Chop House in Newark. He expected, as a reward, to operate as the don of the city, running his Jersey fiefdom as an independent.

"But it was not to be," Natale recounted. "And he later found out it was Carlo Gambino who persuaded the Commission to 'open' the city of Newark."

Caponigro, known for his furious temper, felt the bile rise in his throat as he addressed Salerno with increasing bitterness. "All agreements and promises should be buried with Gambino when they put him in the grave," he snapped. "We owe nothing to that big jerk-off Big Paul, who is a boss only because of his sister's big ass."

Salerno and the other hangers-on were shocked by the crude remark, but he knew that was the least of his concerns with Caponigro. Salerno sipped his martini and considered all the good that had come to him and his friend: Organized crime in Newark was theirs alone, a lucrative mix of gambling, loan-sharking, hijacking goods from the nearby docks and pharmaceutical plants. They kept their stolen stock in a pair of warehouses, like a legitimate retailer. And Freddie was full partner in a jewelry store in Manhattan's Diamond District. Both were, unlikely as it might once have seemed, now millionaires.

Life was good. But Freddie Salerno suddenly had a bad feeling. He sat in silence as the venom dripped from his pal's lips. Salerno had good reason to worry about the thoughts running through Caponigro's head. Salerno had worked as the getaway driver on several hits attributed to Tony Bananas, a mob killer through and through. Caponigro always insisting on pulling the trigger himself, a move that he saw as simple self-preservation: If one of his men did the "work" and felt the rush of taking a life, Tony Bananas might face a rival for control of Newark.

"All the years of watching the life light leave the eyes of the men that he executed only increased his paranoia that another shooter would find killing as easy to do as he had," Natale said. "He was mistaken. Most men must kill because they are ordered to do so. And it was also a requirement for induction into La Cosa Nostra.

"Many of these men dread the thought of ever again being ordered to take a life, unlike Tony Bananas. This was the power he held over everyone else in his regime."

13

One warm spring afternoon in South Philly, Natale swung by Snyder Avenue to visit with the boss. Angelo Bruno had sent word through his partner business partner Raymond "Long John" Martorano, who had just moved into a home about ten minutes away from Natale in New Jersey. The new arrangement allowed Bruno to easily reach out for Natale with no direct contact, his preferred way of doing business.

The trip brought back everything Natale loved about the old neighborhood: blankets, sheets, and bedspreads flapping in the breeze from the second-story windows of the row houses, the new mothers pushing their newborns in strollers down the narrow streets, the sweet smell of the changing seasons in the air. But summer loomed just three months ahead with its stifling heat and humidity, and the boss's wife, Sue, had asked for an air conditioner in the kitchen. Bruno never refused his wife and family anything, and this request was quickly granted.

Natale had never laid eyes on the man installing the unit, a Sicilian immigrant named John Stanfa. Born in a mountain village, Stanfa came to Philadelphia with quite a backstory. A made man on his native island, Stanfa arrived in New York and connected with his relatives in the big city. His nephew John was already a made man in the Gambino family, and his two brothers were major heroin dealers in the South Jersey area.

John Gambino asked his own uncle, Carlo Gambino, for permission to find Stanfa a new home in Philadelphia. Stanfa could provide an inside look at the Bruno family, working as a mole to keep New York abreast of developments down south. Stanfa signed off on the deal; so did Carlo Gambino.

The family boss made a phone call to Bruno, looking to secure a welcoming haven for the new immigrant. Bruno, as customary among the Mafia's dons, welcomed the friend of his friend with open arms.

Stanfa launched a small construction company, financed by Bruno. The Philly boss went a step beyond, instructing all in his family to use Stanfa if they needed any work done.

Natale, after a light and polite knock, was greeted by Sue Bruno. "Is the chief in?" Natale inquired.

"He is." She smiled. "And why are you here so early?"

Natale smiled right back. "When Caesar calls, I come." Sue steered him toward the kitchen and the air-conditioner project. She raised her eyebrows in mock appreciation of the effort, but Natale knew she was flattered that her husband put her concerns first on this fine day. The two men were speaking in Sicilian when Natale found them.

Even before they met, Natale bore a natural distrust toward the Zip—a derogatory term used by the American-born mobsters for their Sicilian-born counterparts. Stanfa was two steps up a ladder as Natale eyed him carefully. The two men were about the same age and the same diminutive size.

The ever-suspicious Natale waited to see what else he would learn about the man in his boss's home.

"This is John Stanfa," said Bruno as the man came down the ladder and toward Natale. "He's good friends with the Gambinos."

Stanfa extended his hand in greeting. Natale, giving the hand an extratight squeeze, stared in the Sicilian's eyes. After years of judging men of all stripes under all kinds of circumstances, Natale didn't like what he saw. He decided Stanfa was an ass-kisser, eager to please on the surface, but dangerous at the core. Natale kept his opinion to himself, instead offering a compliment on the new air conditioner.

Stanfa soon ingratiated himself with Bruno and the rest of the Philadelphia family—particularly consigliere Caponigro and trusted capo Frank Sindone. Underboss Testa was among the few put off by Stanfa's obsequious behavior and servile façade.

The Chicken Man proved more astute than his boss, as Stanfa's true loyalty remained with his cousins in New York. Their unbreakable bonds were forged in the heat of their mountainous Mediterranean home, and a trip across the ocean did nothing to break them. They would instead shatter the family at the other end of the New Jersey Turnpike.

14

Natale was now in his forties, his mob reputation burnished by his work and his future bright, when a legitimate guy—a lawyer, no less—approached him about providing a loan for a South Jersey furniture business somewhat bizarrely named Mr. Living Room. The owner would buy his product at a discount below the Mason-Dixon Line, ship it north, and slap an inflated price tag on every piece.

Natale had the money: By now, he was leasing and running a restaurant inside the Holiday Inn opposite the track. The spot on Route 70 had become a hub of mob business and a clubhouse for the Natale crew, and he held court there most every day.

"Friends of Mr. Bruno—and anybody who was with me—they made a living there," he explained. "You ever play pitching quarters? This is us, inside the restaurant. We're not betting enough across the street! So in between, we pitch quarters for twenty dollars a game. It was fun. It was like kids hanging out in the neighborhood."

But Natale still jumped at the chance to collect easy cash from the furniture salesman. It was a can't-miss operation—until Natale's future in Atlantic City and elsewhere went up in flames.

"The attorney came to me—nice guy, nice family," Natale recounts of his ill-fated investment. "He says, 'By the way, the owner could use a couple hundred thousand to buy some furniture, cheap.'" I said, 'Yeah, okay. How is he, good with the payments? Would you stand for him if he missed?' He said, 'Sure I would.' Okay, good. A couple hundred thousand dollars cash."

A meeting between Ralphy and the owner was arranged; Mr. Living Room turned out to be a guy named Sam. The men shook hands, and Natale explained the particulars of their business arrangement: "This is serious here. Make your payments."

Inevitably, Sam did not. "This, that, the weather, this thing," recalled Natale. The mafioso had a solution to their problem: arson. "I had a crew—the Hatchet, Ronnie Turchi. Forget about it—it would be hard to find out it was arson. I said, 'Do you have insurance? Let me see the insurance policy.'"

The policy was for $1 million. A plan was set in motion. Natale immediately declared that he wanted to double the $200,000 loan for his troubles, unless he decided that taking half of the million-dollar payout was more appropriate for the aggravation. The only bump in the road, as far as Natale could see, was the guard dog left in the store every night.

"I told him, 'We're gonna set this place on fire. Make sure the dog ain't in the building that night, 'cause if the dog's inside, I'm gonna be angry,'" Natale recalled. The dog was spared, and Mr. Living Room was torched. Everything looked good until an insurance adjuster came to interview Sam—who caved under questioning.

"This guy comes up, for some reason there's an argument," Natale recalled of the conversation that caused his downfall. "Sam says, 'I think there's been an arson. And I've been doing things with [the arsonists] for a long time. To the insurance guy! And that was the end of that.

"That's how we all got indicted. What do I know? He was making money off the arson. I could have rammed my head into a wall. I got twelve years on that, but I was out on bail."

Which gave Natale a chance to visit sunny Florida. On the whole, to paraphrase W. C. Fields, he was far better off in Philadelphia: good weather and bad luck awaited.

The arson bust, while in no way a blessing, was hardly the curse that Natale initially feared. The murders of McGreal and Feeney remained unsolved. An arson charge was a comparatively minor blip on Natale's crooked highway. The initial gut punch of the possible twelve-year sentence waned as new business prospects cropped up.

"It was a shock, twelve years—son of a bitch!" he said. "I got jammed up. What was I gonna do? It wasn't a big deal, not to me, because I thought they knew some of the things that would put me away for the rest of my life. At that time, I woulda done five, six years. By the time I get into shape, I'll be home."

Natale was out on bail pending his appeal when another lucrative opportunity knocked in the person of his old nemesis Charlie Allen, accompanied by one of Ralphy's cousins—Raymond Bernard, the son of his beloved aunt

Dolly. Bernard was married with kids and had a penchant for gambling—and losing.

"A printer by trade," Natale says now. "And a gambler and conniver by choice."

The proposal was a moneymaking drug deal for half a million quaaludes and ten kilos of cocaine.

"I, being the bighearted man that I am—it's my cousin, right?" he said. "Money was easy with me. I'm making it, doing a thousand things. Raymond says, 'Please, Ralphy.' And my aunt—she was always good to me."

It sounded promising, but Natale was blinded by the cash and in the dark about his partners. Allen was now in his third year working as a confidential informant for the Philadelphia office of the FBI. He had agreed one year earlier to become a federal witness after his arrest for running a meth lab with Bernard in Swampoodle. Bernard flipped, too, with both men promised a walk if they cooperated in a sting targeting Natale.

"They get a little house in the Irish neighborhood," Natale related. "Of course, they're trying to make meth—it blows up. It's very volatile, that stuff. They fucking get caught. The cops say, 'Charlie, you don't have to worry.' They set him up because they thought, 'We gotta get Ralphy off the streets because of Atlantic City, we don't want him there.'

"Charlie was a rat to begin with. I heard when he came home from Lewisburg, he went to the FBI and said, 'I need money. I'll be a confidential informant.' An agent told me that! And that's the end of that."

Allen handled the introductions of all parties involved. His partners were Drug Enforcement Administration undercovers. Negotiations were done on a forty-two-foot yacht moored in sunny Florida. Natale was aboard when the bust came down at 6:00 a.m. on February 8, 1979; he walked off the luxury boat and into a pair of handcuffs.

"Where was I gonna be?" he asks now with a sly grin. "A seedy motel?"

But there was no denying how sharply the DEA sting, arranged by a blood relative and a mob associate from his hometown, stung Natale.

"They set me up!" he said, still irate forty years later. "I felt sorry for them. They got caught up in something. I felt pity for them. I went down to Florida, I'm on the boat: 'Don't worry, the money's there.' Boom! The next thing I know, I'm locked up. Forget about it. It was crazy. It really was."

The FBI simultaneously descended on his suburban New Jersey home. Natale, generally a live-and-let-die kind of guy, still nurtures a grudge against one of the FBI agents who kicked in the front and back doors in Pennsauken, where Lucia was inside with two of their daughters—ages eight and fifteen. The agents waved their guns in front of the trio, who minutes earlier were baking cookies.

An agent discovered Natale's cache of hidden hollow-points and approached Lucia, who was standing with her younger girl.

"That's what your husband does," the agent announced. "These bullets are for an assassin. Your husband is an assassin."

Natale's ire rises at the thought: "My eight-year-old, she never forgot that to this day. And my wife just looked at him: 'You had to say that right in front of her?'"

A second grudge rose from the arrest: the blood betrayal by Cousin Ray still rankles Ralph: "Jesus Christ, my own cousin! Why didn't he tell me the day before, 'I can't do it, they're setting you up.' The whole world would have changed. Everything would be different. But it wasn't. It is what it is."

The FBI's thinking was simple. Natale, out on bail in the other case, would immediately go to prison once the new charges were known. This would give the feds a chance to lean on Natale with some leverage, working their way up the family hierarchy in an attempt to finally take down Angelo Bruno.

The jailing instead offered Bruno's enemy an unimpeded path to take down the Docile Don.

Natale immediately knew this was a major jackpot. Combined with the arson case, this meant he was facing— for the first time, after thirty years in organized crime—a seriously lengthy time in lockdown.

"When I got arrested in Florida, I said, 'This is gonna be a long one for me.' But it was everything else but the murders. They all thought I did those, but they had no proof. As the old cowboys say, 'Dead men tell no tales.'"

Natale made three decisions going into the uncharted future: He was no rat. He wouldn't give up shit to anyone about anything. And he was now a vegetarian.

As he sat inside the Lauderhill jail after his arrest, the guards brought in bologna-and-cheese sandwiches for the prisoners awaiting processing. Natale asked for one sandwich, hold the bologna. And he hasn't had a piece of meat since.

The next morning, Natale was summoned by a corrections officer at the Lauderhill city jail. Two FBI agents were waiting to make his acquaintance.

"Listen to them," the captain advised. "They're good guys."

The pitch was short: They wanted Angelo Bruno. And they wanted Ralph Natale to serve him up on a silver platter.

Natale's head was suddenly swimming. "In my mind, at that time, I'm worried about my wife. They went in my house, broke down all the walls, looking for money and guns. They had just grabbed me off the boat—the change of culture at that moment, you'll never feel that. You're living like a human being, and then you're—*boom!* Like a dog."

His priorities changed quickly as the two agents started talking. "You wanna talk about pressure? They put a list down: 'Take a look at these names. You recognize any of these names?'"

Natale recognized them as victims from Philadelphia mob killings. He quickly realized this was more than a simple drug case, and prosecutors from Florida to Philadelphia to Chicago and New York had an interest in his prosecution.

The taller of the two finally spoke. "Ralphy, we know that you either killed these people personally or with others on orders from Angelo Bruno, Carlo Gambino, or Tony Accardo. All you have to do is become a federal witness against these men, and all of your problems with the law will go away. Tell us who ordered these killings, and you won't have to spend a night in jail."

Outwardly, Natale's demeanor remained calm as the agent addressed him. Inside, one thought ran through his head: "These sons of bitches are gonna try and bury me."

Natale didn't waste his time or his breath: "You got the wrong guy. Captain, put me back in my cell."

The parting words of one agent rang in his ears: "You'll be back."

Natale was convicted on three counts, each with a twenty-five-year term—but was expecting a much more lenient sentence on a simple drug bust, especially after dodging charges for his other mob sins. Then prosecutors tried to sentence him under the Dangerous Special Offender Act, putting him in line for a life sentence.

Natale, while not surprised, was outraged. "I ain't a rapist," he snapped. "I ain't a serial killer."

Back in Philadelphia, Bruno reached out for an old friend: his trusted lawyer, Kossman. The boss and the semiretired barrister were client and lawyer, but they were much more—the two men socialized and played the stock market together.

"Ang said, 'You gotta go save his ass,'" Natale remembers. "He knew: they wanted him! They woulda gave me anything. But he knew I wouldn't give them shit."

The lawyer—whose clients also included Blinky Palermo—headed south. A special hearing dragged across three contentious days, with lots of legal wrangling as Natale nervously awaited his fate.

"Imagine that!" he snaps. "I was never arrested, even for an assault. Put me in front of a judge as a dangerous special offender? The prosecutors put in that I did this, or I did that. No evidence! After the second day, the judge said, 'Do you have any more? Do you have any evidence?' Thank God. Suppose he said, 'This little dago bastard, I'll bury him.'"

Once Kossman worked a little legal legerdemain, Ralph Natale was sentenced to fifteen years by a judge who almost apologized for the draconian sentence. The time would run consecutively with the twelve years waiting back north for the Mr. Living Room blaze.

The federal guidelines for his criminal convictions were fifty-two months to eighty months—a shade short of seven years. He was instead facing twenty-seven years, and Natale was stunned by the severity of the sentences.

"Oh my God, they buried me," he said. "Wouldn't give me parole, wouldn't give me nothing. I lost everything I had on the street. It cost me all my homes, and it almost cost me my family. I could cry when I think of it. My eyes were full of tears when I went into court, thinking about it."

He was shipped by bus, shackled with leg irons, linked to forty other inmates by a waist chain, and then thrown into solitary confinement. But Natale was nothing if not resilient. He was soon confident he could do the time, and he was pleased to see an assortment of familiar faces behind bars.

"When I went into prison, I was held in high regard because of what I did on the street," he said. "When I first arrived, every made man treated me with respect."

With his jail time came plenty of time to reflect on life, and Natale pondered what was going on back home. He was troubled by what he'd seen and sensed in the Bruno regime before heading down to Florida after his own pinpoint in time with Charlie Allen. Something about Caponigro and Sindone made him feel hinky.

"Tony was courting Sindone, and through Sindone, John Stanfa," Natale recounted. "But if I had said anything to Ang about their sudden closeness at that time, he would have flown into a rage. Imagine anyone talking about his consigliere and one of his most trusted capos!"

Time would tell that Natale's assessment was deadly accurate.

15

With Ralphy off the streets for a good long time, things were changing in Philadelphia—mostly because of the man in Newark, Caponigro. The festering bitterness inside Tony Bananas bubbled and bubbled until he decided it was time to take action. Natale felt it was no coincidence that the turmoil took place with him imprisoned far from home.

"That's what Tony Bananas was waiting for," he said. "Not that he was afraid of me. But he was afraid I might kill him. He knew how I was. As soon as I heard it, I would know where it would come from. I'd go right to that bar he had in Newark. And I would bring my crew with me. I'd bring the Hachet—Mike Marrone—and Ronnie Turchi, a killer. But Mike and Ronnie got arrested first, a couple of months before me.

"When I was home, when Skinny was alive, nobody would even look at Angelo Bruno. Skinny would kill 'em right there. And when they took out me and my little crew, the door was wide-open. They didn't wait long. They put it together. They talked to goddamn Frank Sindone. I shoulda killed him. Another jerk-off. Him and Nicky Scarfo."

The plot to murder Angelo Bruno required the treachery of two mob families in the two cities at either end of the New Jersey Turnpike. While Caponigro angled to replace Bruno as boss, the mighty Genovese family saw an opportunity to extend its influence in the Garden State—and perhaps as far south as Atlantic City.

Caponigro had surreptitiously reached out to his Genovese equivalent, consigliere Frank "Funzi" Tieri. The unusual request, made only after careful consideration, was delivered in a blanket of secrecy. Caponigro knew the topic would bring repercussions from Philadelphia to the Big Apple to the Outfit in Chicago.

The Genovese family was in ascent since the death of Carlo Gambino and the rise of its own powerful leader in Vincent "the Chin" Gigante—a brilliant mob mind who hid his light beneath a ratty bathrobe and floppy cap. The Chin posed as a mental patient, checking himself in and out of a psychiatric hospital, to successfully dodge prosecution for decades.

The 1966 pact between Chicago, the Gambinos, and Philadelphia left the Genovese family on the outside looking in when the casinos opened down the Jersey Shore. It also left a bad taste in the mouths of outflanked family leaders, a bone of contention that never disappeared.

Caponigro intended to exploit the situation for his own benefit. His friend and driver Freddie Salerno drove his boss from Newark to the Triangle Civic Improvement Association, the dingy Sullivan Street social club that served as Gigante's headquarters in Greenwich Village. A pair of thick-necked goons quickly steered Tony Bananas inside the small storefront heavy with the smell of good cigars and better coffee.

Tieri was waiting for him. Caponigro pondered his pitch to open the door for both the Genovese and himself by murdering the Docile Don. Tieri led his visitor to a table in the rear of the cramped, no-frills club, where the two men sat at a thick-legged table to talk. Espresso was served, and the two mob veterans began their verbal bobbing and weaving, the conversation like a showdown between two fighters.

It soon became clear that Caponigro was punching above his weight class. And in his bloodlust to fill Bruno's shoes, he seemingly forgot a previous beef over a bookie operation claimed as his own by both Funzi and the Philly consigliere. The dispute had gone before the Commission, and Caponigro was declared the winner.

Tieri, still nursing a grudge, decided this was the time to gain a cruel measure of vengeance—and regain control of the North Jersey turf.

"Tony Bananas was, in his own right, a cunning and devious mafioso," said Natale. "But not in the class of Funzi Tieri when it came to Machiavellian tactics. Old Niccolò Machiavelli could have taken lessons from the elder statesman of the Genovese family."

Caponigro asked about boss Gigante by rubbing his chin and asking about "our friend"—standard procedure when discussing the permanently paranoid Genovese boss, who barred one and all from using the name. Tieri offered a half smile in return before asking, "How are all of our friends in Philadelphia?" Tony Bananas was thrilled when Tieri didn't mention Bruno by name, taking the omission as a sign that he was on the right track. Caponigro then ranted for more than an hour about the situation in Philly, about the unholy marriage of the Gambino family to his family in Atlantic City.

Tieri finally leaned over to respond, his voice a hiss: "Do what you have to do."

Those six words set in motion a calamitous and cruel series of events that left three Mafia dons dead in five years, dozens of soldiers slain, and two mob families in total disarray.

"Funzi Tieri played Tony Bananas like a Stradivarius," Natale said. "He used Tony's own treachery to anesthetize his cunning and awareness to the hidden Genovese agenda."

Caponigro and Tieri hugged before the Jersey guy headed home, totally unaware that he was a pawn in a deadly game run by the New Yorker. Tony Bananas, with his steps urgent and his face dead serious, marched toward the big black sedan where Salerno was waiting.

"As soon as we get to our joint, call [Sindone] and tell him we're coming in tonight for dinner about seven p.m.," Caponigro announced. "Felix and Meats are coming with us. And tell him he'll be drinking champagne after he hears what I've got to tell him."

When the pair arrived thirty minutes later at Caponigro's bar, Down Neck, in Newark, Tony "Meats" Ferrante and "Little Felix" Bocchino were drinking at the bar. Natale was unsurprised by their inclusion in the plot: "Well, they were strutting way before the killing, when I was on the street, before I went away. They did little things, hijackings, and then big things—this scheme, that scheme, they were big schemers. Tony Meats was the blood nephew to Tony Bananas, so he became somebody. And Felix was with him, so he became somebody. Eventually, Tony Bananas made them."

Ferrante and Bocchino once went as far as proposing a

hit on Blinky Palermo after a couple of business deals went bad. They arrived at the Rickshaw Inn for a meeting with Natale to lay out their plan.

"They said, 'Ralph, you got pretty close with Blinky, didn't you?' Normally I would say, 'None of your fucking business.' I didn't like their tone already, but if you respond too fast with men like that, they won't tell you the rest," Natale recalled. "They said he fucked up a couple of deals, and they were going to kill him."

Natale had heard enough. He looked at Ferrante, and then at Bocchino. Natale rose slowly and leaned in close to his guests.

"If you even breathe hard near Blinky Palermo, I will kill you," he seethed. "I'll kill you right here if you fucking say a word. I'll fucking kill the both of you."

The death threat was enough to scare the pair off. The two mobsters survived to plot another murder—the killing of Angelo Bruno.

Caponigro, his team of treachery assembled, set the wheels of his high-wire act of murder in motion. The weapon, it was decided, would be a shotgun imported from Newark—no hardware with a link to Philly. The consigliere feared a stop on the New Jersey Turnpike if he transported the weapon himself, and so Bocchino and Ferrante were entrusted with delivering the gun to Philadelphia.

The pair brought the murder weapon to a slaughterhouse on Front Street. Bocchino brought the gun to an upstairs office to break it down, make sure all the parts were in working order, and then reassemble the instrument of death.

To Natale, the plot was another example—reminiscent of the late Joe McGreal—of people trying to be something they were not. "They wanted to change their destinies, from common thugs to somebodies," he reflected years later. That trip required more than a shotgun and a black heart.

All sorts of destinies were recharted by the time the Caponigro cabal was finished on March 21, 1980.

Caponigro and Salerno traveled south together on their mission, arriving at the Philly home of capo Sindone just off the first exit after the Walt Whitman Bridge. The front door was unlocked, and the men exchanged handshakes, hugs, and kisses on the cheek. This was the type of respect that Caponigro craved—and expected—once Bruno was gone.

The Docile Don had forbidden such greetings between made men, feeling it was an ostentatious display of what was supposed to be a secret society. The only exceptions were when meeting goodfellas from New York, where such hellos were de rigueur, and for mob initiation ceremonies.

The display in Sindone's living room was a repudiation of Bruno and his ways. The underboss served coffee as the traitors discussed the ultimate betrayal of their benevolent boss. Sindone then produced a plate of anise-flavored biscotti, a favorite of Caponigro as the capo ingratiated himself with the man who would be king.

The reverie was interrupted by another knock on the door, and John Stanfa entered. The Sicilian-born mobster was the key player in the murder plot, the linchpin of their evil. It was a particularly cruel twist: Bruno's old friend Gambino had vouched for Stanfa, giving his stamp of approval to the Sicilian. And now he was conspiring to kill the man who'd welcomed him.

Bruno had unhesitatingly taken care of this Judas, unaware of the duplicity in his heart. Loyalty and honor, the founding precepts of Italian organized crime, were trumped once more by greed, jealousy, and the heartbeat of blind ambition.

Stanfa, unbeknownst to his coconspirators, had already reached out to his Gambino associates in New York. He was simply following the code of his native island: promise everyone, but trust no one. The rituals of handshakes, hugs, and kisses was repeated in Sindone's home. Stanfa took things one step further: as if on the set of a movie, he took Caponigro's hand and kissed that, too.

"Don Antonio," he said in Sicilian, "I give you my life."

It was an Oscar-winning moment, played to the hilt by Stanfa for an appreciative audience of one—Tony Bananas. With the formalities done, the four sat down to discuss the specifics of their plan to murder a man who had helped every one of the quartet during his reign.

16

Angelo Bruno woke up that same morning, kissed his wife of nearly a half century good-bye, and walked out the front door. It was the last time the couple would ever speak.

"You look so handsome in that blue business suit," she told him as he exited, her final words to her beloved spouse. Bruno met with his lawyer pal Kossman for lunch, business as usual.

That evening, Bruno headed to Torano's Italian Bar and Restaurant, owned by none other than Frank Sindone and situated just two blocks from the market. The crowd grew thick as word of Bruno's impending arrival spread, with an assortment of mob wannabes eager for a glimpse of the boss. A nervous Sindone sipped on a martini poured into a coffee cup; even on the night when he planned to murder Bruno, he did not want the teetotaler boss to see him drinking hard liquor.

Ralph Natale sat cluelessly in a Florida prison as the night's events unspooled.

Bruno's presence at Torano's was intended to soothe hard

feelings within his family. Sindone and underboss Testa had had a falling-out over business, and the boss wanted to set things right. Earlier in the day, Testa volunteered to join the two men for dinner. Bruno believed this issue was best handled by himself alone, a response that left the Chicken Man uneasy.

Decades later, Natale remains astounded that Testa failed to connect the murderous dots pointing directly at the boss. "Phil Testa was as dumb as they come," he sniped. "He didn't see what was going on with Caponigro and Sindone. He should have sensed something wasn't right. If Skinny Razor was around, they all would have been gone before anybody got close to Ang. He would have seen it, sensed it, smelled it. But Testa was a dunce. He was dim-witted. And what happened, happened."

Testa meekly obeyed his mentor and benefactor, who had ruled unchallenged for so long after plucking him from the obscurity of a butcher's shop. "I'll see you tomorrow," said Testa before Bruno headed toward the car where his driver awaited.

John Stanfa started the engine and delivered Bruno to the restaurant.

Sindone, who had ascended from small-time dope dealer to millionaire during Bruno's reign, hustled across the room when his boss entered through a side entrance. As Natale heard it, Sindone nearly made a fatal error: He started to embrace Bruno, a move guaranteed to set off the careful boss's internal alarm system. Sindone caught himself and instead offered a handshake of pure betrayal. He then led Bruno to a table for his last supper.

The two men ate and talked. The chain-smoking Bruno went back to his waiting vehicle, lighting another of his ever-present cigarettes. Stanfa would typically lower the passenger-side window an inch or two to let the boss's cigarette smoke waft into the night. Instead, Stanfa had let the window down about halfway before they drove through the misty night toward Bruno's row house on Snyder Avenue. The boss never noticed the difference, and the car would soon become his coffin.

"He trusted everybody around him too much," Natale observed with hindsight.

Lying in wait was the ruthless Caponigro, who'd decided to handle the execution personally, hoisting himself into the top spot with a single blast from the shotgun that he cradled in his arms. Bruno's car eased into a spot outside the home where the boss had bid his wife farewell only hours before.

Caponigro emerged from the darkness and put the barrel against Bruno's right ear. So came the violent end to the Docile Don, longtime padrone of the Philadelphia La Cosa Nostra. The sound of the blast echoed across the quiet streets, and throughout the world of organized crime. Neighbors and the simply curious rushed onto Snyder Avenue as the sounds of sirens filled the night.

Sue Bruno knew what the sound meant, and she wept inside their home for her husband.

John Stanfa—imagine the good fortune—escaped with just a few stray pellets in his arm. He was taken to a nearby hospital, with Bruno's body left in the open for all to see inside the car spattered with his blood.

Caponigro climbed into a waiting getaway car headed for Newark, his bloodthirsty work for the evening now done. Freddie Salerno was behind the wheel. "I waited over twenty years to do it," Tony Bananas reflected. "When Carlo died, it was only a matter of time."

Bocchino and Ferrante broke the shotgun back into parts and dumped the weapon into the Delaware River near the foot of the Walt Whitman Bridge. The pair climbed into Ferrante's Mercury Marquis and drove to a preplanned rendezvous at Caponigro's condo. Only now, when the deed was done, did the consequences of the plot begin to play out in their minds.

Sindone, in his dark-colored Eldorado, made the same northern pilgrimage, his ghoulish features awash in the green glow of the dashboard. He rode alone, accompanied only by the promise of a slot as underboss in the new Caponigro regime. As with Bocchino and Ferrante, the fallout from the killing was suddenly in the forefront of his thoughts.

The worst of those scenarios: What if Tieri had suckered them all into a Sicilian scam from which there was no escape—at least while breathing. Sindone finally arrived at Caponigro's posh four-bedroom condo with its views of the sprawling New York skyline. The Newark capo was waiting, along with the rest of the plotters: Salerno, Ferrante, and Bocchino.

Ferrante asked about the one person missing: Stanfa, who was taken to a Philadelphia hospital and would face a grilling by the feds and local cops.

"That Zip's got more balls than that whole crew of Testa's," Caponigro sneered. "He knows what to do. Remember, he's the only live witness to what was done."

Tony Bananas poured everyone a drink and made plans to contact Tieri about the pot of gold at the end of their bloody red rainbow.

Testa was warming up a leftover veal cutlet when the door of his home in the posh Girard Estates flew open. His son Salvie burst inside, barely able to utter the words that now poured from his mouth: "Dad, they killed Ang." The young man could barely breathe as he delivered the news. All the color had drained from Salvie's face as his father stood in their kitchen.

The two had bonded as the Chicken Man's wife battled unsuccessfully against cancer. Her death left father and son living alone in the house with its stone front and welcoming porch. Salvie wanted to deliver the news personally to his dad, but he had another motive for coming home: he wanted to make sure that Phil Testa was not next on the hit parade.

"Who?" shouted the elder Testa. "And where?" Only then did he notice that Salvie was accompanied by his whole crew of young hoods.

The son provided the details: Outside Bruno's house. The cops had left the bloody corpse of the boss sitting inside the car. "They left him there for everybody to see, the motherfuckers," said Salvie. "The greaseball [Stanfa] was driving him."

His father's spit out his venomous reply: "That no-good motherfucker. He was in on it, or else they would have killed him, too." Testa then instructed his son to call Nicky Scarfo in Atlantic City and assemble the city's made men at the Hilton Hotel near the old Veterans Stadium.

"Make sure, Salvie, they come loaded," the father commanded as he slipped on a trench coat. "Those cocksuckers really did it."

Before Phil Testa could leave, Chuckie Merlino—a Scarfo loyalist—burst into the house. Nicky had sent him to protect the underboss, and Nicky was already on his way to the city. Scarfo's nephew Phil Leonetti and Nicky "the Blade" Virgilio were with him. They were headed for Merlino's home, where his son Joey was waiting for further instructions.

A crowd was now gathering outside the home of the presumed new boss, unaware of the machinations that had led to this night. It was as if they half expected Testa to emerge like a politician on election night and deliver a statement. Most fully expected the blast that had killed Bruno would not be the last volley fired by the Philly family, now under the direction of the man inside the house.

The first silent shot was fired by Scarfo from a pay phone in a rest stop off the Atlantic City Expressway. He pulled a small, leatherbound phone book from his pocket and dialed the number of Bobby Manna, an old friend from the Genovese family in New York. The two had done time together in the early seventies for refusing to speak at a New Jersey hearing on organized crime. A mutual respect and friendship was forged inside the walls of a South Jersey prison where the two men spent hours walking in the yard and talking quite candidly about their lives and The Life.

Upon their release, Manna shared this phone number with the Brooklyn-born Scarfo. If Little Nicky needed anything, Manna advised, he was reachable 24–7. The Blade, over Scarfo's initial objection, stood guard as his boss made the call. Another pinpoint in time.

It was a calculated gamble by Scarfo, as the details of the Bruno killing were yet to shake out. The Commission would decide who would pay for the assassination. Scarfo's mind cleared when he heard Manna's voice on the other end of the line.

Manna was expecting the call because of Tieri's conniving

chat with Caponigro months before. The two New Yorkers saw the Bruno hit as the chance for the rising Genovese family, under the guidance of the Chin, to grab their piece of the New Jersey rackets. The agreement on Atlantic City was now a deal between two dead men: Gambino and Bruno.

Manna invited Scarfo to bring Testa with him for a breakfast meeting in New York, 7:00 a.m., at his place. He hung up abruptly, feeling no need to wait for a reply. The connection to the Genovese family gave Scarfo a leg up on the new boss, Testa, as Little Nicky exercised his "in" with the New Yorkers.

Scarfo was already angling to play Brutus to the Chicken Man's Caesar. Testa and Scarfo were headed to the city before sunrise the next morning. Gambino boss Castellano would send his own man down to Philadelphia to get the lay of the land, unaware that the Genovese family had beaten him to the punch.

Word of the assassination soon reached the Federal Correctional Facility in Homestead, Florida, where Natale was held in a special unit known as the Glass House—an homage to a prison within a prison, with walls of bulletproof glass. The space was reserved for mobsters and other inmates deemed high-security risks.

The first-floor recreation area, with its pool table and television, had closed at 10:00 p.m. on March 21. Ralphy had returned to his cubicle and slipped into a restless sleep. At around 11:00 p.m. Gambino family associate Frankie Verna appeared, his voice as soft as his news was harsh.

"Ralphy, wake up," Verna whispered. "Take it easy. I just heard on the radio. They killed your friend."

That moment stayed with Natale through the rest of his

time behind bars, and even to this day: "I could see his face now. He came and told me, 'I just heard some news.' 'Your friend'—I knew who he meant right away."

Natale regained his composure and asked if there were any details: Was anyone seen after the murder? Any arrests? Any details?

Verna saw the suddenly angry Natale rise and head toward the prison phones, which recorded all inmate conversations. He urged the hotheaded Natale to take some time before calling anybody or saying something that might raise the hackles of those listening to the tapes.

"I'll go make some coffee," said Verna. The two men sat in Natale's cubicle for the rest of a long, sad night.

A frustrated Natale was unable to strike back at the killers of his friend and boss, even as his mind and soul screamed for vengeance. The impotence was crippling. "I felt like I wasn't a human being," said Natale. "I couldn't do anything that a man could do. That's how I felt. I called the next morning to my wife."

As the phone rang back in Pennsauken, New Jersey, Natale's mind began racing—his head suddenly filled with the sound and fury of the opening lap of the Indy 500. One name kept surfacing through the confusion: Tony Caponigro. Lucia picked up after just two rings, and Natale—without so much as a "good morning"—began to speak rapid-fire. "What are they saying on the TV?"

After a quick news update, Natale provided his wife with specific directions: "Lucia, there are two things I want you to do for me. First, call Long John. The numbers are in our personal directory. Tell him to be at the Centani at one o'clock this afternoon. Secondly, take [sons] Michael and Frankie with you to the wake. Lucia, I'll talk to you after I speak to Long John. Don't worry. Everything will be okay."

He hung up without saying good-bye.

At 1:00 p.m., Natale was back on the prison phone dialing the number at the Italian restaurant where he was a partner with the current head of Local 170, Charlie DeRose—who picked up after a single ring. Without small talk DeRose handed the phone to Martorano. FBI agents had trailed Bruno's longtime sidekick to the restaurant this afternoon.

"What a terrible thing last night, our friend," said Long John, his voice sounding uneasy to Natale. Martorano, knowing every word was being recorded, was about to declare his innocence in the hit for the unseen listeners who would review their conversation.

Natale interrupted, snapping, "Listen, my friend was killed. So don't play silly games with me. I am in no fucking mood. This is being recorded here, so don't pretend that it's not what it is. Those two motherfuckers did it, didn't they?"

There was a long pause once Natale had pointed the finger directly at Caponigro and Sindone. "How did you know that from down there where you're at?" asked a perplexed Martorano, setting off an eruption from the other end of the phone.

"You dumb motherfuckers!" Natale raged. "Nobody was even near my friend when he died! The shame is on your souls, starting with Testa and Scarfo."

Martorano's explanation, that Bruno had asked Testa to steer clear of the sit-down, fell on deaf ears.

"Jerk-offs!" Natale ranted. "Why didn't Phil send some of his crew to babysit Ang until he got home? I wonder why not. Well, fuck them all! Somebody's got to pay for this, and if it takes a hundred years, I'll make sure of it. Longy, if you hear anything else on this, tell my wife at the wake. I'll talk to you after that."

Natale slammed down the phone, sending a message from Florida: he was unsure of Martorano's role, if any, in the slaughter of their mutual friend.

17

THE WAKE

Lucia was home on the day of Bruno's wake when the phone rang again. She answered to hear the voice of Bruno's long-time business partner Martorano. Don't wait in the line at the funeral home, he told her, but come to the front and look for him. Lucia and her sons, Michael and Frankie, would be escorted directly inside, where Sue Bruno wanted a few minutes with the wife of her slain husband's imprisoned loyalist.

Thousands of mourners—a mix of family and the Family, made men and mob wannabes, all flanked by the merely curious—snaked along the sidewalk outside the Pennsylvania Burial Company on South Broad Street. Inside, the hundreds of floral arrangements included ten carloads of orchids alone. It was a scene straight out of *The Godfather,* playing out in South Philly.

"There is no wake like an Italian wake," Natale said. "It's as if the Colosseum in Rome was open for business after two thousand years. Here was the wake the South Philadelphians had waited for, a chance to pay homage to their Caesar,

Angelo Bruno. This was their chance to mingle with the made men of the Philadelphia Mafia that they read about in the *Philadelphia Inquirer* and the *Daily News*."

While the wake had the feel of a once-in-a-lifetime event, the future would prove that feeling was untrue.

Lucia and her sons, with Michael at the wheel, were stuck in the massive traffic jam paralyzing the local streets. They finally found a parking space and started walking to the wake, with Lucia showing her two sons the old dressmaking business where she once worked as a teen. The mother was dressed all in black, the sons in dark suits with black ties, as they grimly approached the funeral home.

Long John spotted Lucia and the boys, steering the trio through a crowd that parted quickly at the sight of Mrs. Natale. The first five rows of seats near the ornate casket were filled with mafiosi as the Natales inched toward the kneeler, where they would say one final prayer for the soul of Angelo Bruno.

Bruno's only son, Michael, a man of the legitimate world, moved to bring Lucia to the empty seat alongside his mother, Sue. Mrs. Natale first put two fingers to her lips, then touched the slain boss's forehead—a farewell from the absent Ralphy, so furious and powerless in the wake of the murder.

Sue Bruno stood to greet Lucia, who softly told her friend to sit. Sue's hands were cold, dry, and trembling as Lucia took them in her own hands. When the two women locked eyes, they broke down in tears and embraced.

Lucia spoke first. "My Ralphy sends you his heart, and no matter what or who, they will pay."

"Lucia," replied Sue, "just sit a couple of minutes with me until I get myself together, and then I must tell you a few things."

Lucia nodded yes, maintained the embrace, and scoured the room with her eyes as her husband would have done. Standing to the right of the casket was the Chicken Man, Testa, flanked by his demented followers Little Nicky Scarfo, Crazy Phil Leonetti, and Chuckie Merlino. The next generation of the Philly Mafia stood close behind: Testa's son Salvie, Scarfo's son Nicky Jr., and Merlino's son Joey.

Lucia was struck with a single thought: these men were the enemies of her husband. And then another one: the men mourning Angelo Bruno were men of no substance, unworthy of filling the Docile Don's shoes. Her reveries were interrupted by the sound of Sue Bruno's voice.

"Lucia, please don't take this the wrong way, but I must say these things to you. I am glad your husband is in prison, only because if he wasn't, he would be laid out next to my Angelo. They would have had to kill Ralphy with my Angelo. 'Cause if they didn't, your Ralphy would have made the streets of South Philly run red with their blood."

Lucia was somewhat surprised by the blunt comment, as it was the first time anyone had spoken what she knew was true of her husband, her teenage sweetheart and the father of their children. A weeping Sue warned Lucia that the stunning hit would turn their worlds upside down.

"Tell Ralphy that everything will change for him because of what happened to my Angelo," Sue Bruno declared as tears streamed down her face. "And tell him my family sends its love and respect."

Lucia said good-bye, promising to stop by after the burial. Her two sons kissed the widow on her cheek and followed their mother out past Testa and the rest. As they nodded toward her in a friendly way, Lucia felt the hostility coming off the group in waves—from the pockmarked face of Testa and the ferretlike glare of Scarfo. She went home and booked a flight to Florida for the morning after the funeral. She would tell her husband every word, every detail, every message both stated and inferred.

The words of Sue Bruno echoed in her head, and Lucia knew she needed to pass the message along. The generosity of the Bruno regime would be buried along with the murdered boss. The timing was terrible: Lucia, alone with her five kids, was dependent on the cash-filled envelope that had come regularly from Bruno to cover her expenses with her husband behind bars.

The new boss, Phil "Chicken Man" Testa, cut off the cash flow shortly after assuming the throne. Natale became even more enraged, with his anger extending to Testa's newly appointed underboss Scarfo. He felt the resurrected Atlantic City mobster's influence already seeping poison into the family.

Natale, by now transferred to the federal prison in Lewisburg, Pennsylvania, finally sent a message back to Philadelphia's new mob leaders, expressing his disgust at the decision to leave his family flat. Testa and Scarfo summoned Martorano to deliver their response. He met with Lucia, and Long John nervously repeated the message word for word: "Tell your husband that we can reach him anywhere. Even in Lewisburg."

The next day, Lucia and daughter Carmen made the three-hour drive from Philadelphia to the prison. Just as Martorano had, she recounted the twelve-word threat. She knew even before Ralph opened his mouth exactly what her husband would say.

"Lucia, call Long John and tell him to meet you tomorrow morning in front of the ShopRite"—just a short walk from their home in Pennsauken. "And tell Long John to bring this message back to Phil Testa and Nicky Scarfo. Tell them to do what they have to do, because when I come home, I am going to see the both of them." Natale then looked directly in his wife's face before finishing. "When you're finished telling that scum what I said, turn around and walk away, and never, never meet with anyone again."

Natale's only bit of comfort came from a single thought: revenge is a dish best served cold. He had fifteen years left behind bars, and the thought marinated into an obsession. A plan was already coalescing in his mind, where it would stay for another decade. Natale laid out his plan to Philip "Rusty" Rastelli, the imprisoned head of the Bonanno family, as they walked through the prison yard.

"Philly Rastelli was a real man. He asked to see me the first morning I was there," Natale recounted. "I never met him on the street. He said, 'Hi, Ralphy—I'm Phil Rastelli.' We shook hands through the bars. I was the only guy he would walk with in that yard. Then we get into it a little bit, and he said, 'Is it true? You're just starting this bit?'

"I said, 'I can't lie to you, 'cause you're like the men who broke me in. When I go back, when I get back there, I'm taking back what was mine, because they took what was mine. And they took what belonged to Ang, and they didn't give nothing to my wife. All due respect to you, because I know who you are. I don't give a fuck who says no. I'm gonna do it.'"

Natale believed nothing short of his own death would stop him from turning those words into reality.

Ralph felt that he knew exactly why the Chicken Man, along with his new consigliere, Scarfo, abruptly ended the promised payments to Lucia.

"Why would he fuck with me?" Natale asked rhetorically. "He figured I was gonna get buried. I'm dead. Knowing me, knowing my temper, he thinks I'm never gonna see him again. He thought he was safe."

The killing of Bruno unleashed a cascade of bloodshed, as if someone had pulled his finger from the dike of festering jealously and greed that had built during Bruno's long reign atop the family. Among the first to die were the minor-league Machiavellis behind the Bruno hit, their fates determined immediately by the mob's ruling Commission: everyone must die.

The death sentences were meant both as retribution for the killing of one of their own and a harsh reminder to one and all that the unsanctioned murder of a boss violated one of the Mafia's most sacrosanct laws. Even if the murder was done with a wink and nod of approval from within.

The Genovese family, when the Commission met to discuss the Bruno murder, immediately volunteered to exact vengeance for the hit. It was a brilliant move—the very family that cleverly put the whole mess in motion would now clean things up, insuring that Caponigro would never get a chance to tell the story of his meeting with Tieri or plead his case with one of the other four bosses. Tony Bananas remained clueless about his fate, unaware that he had unwittingly signed his own death warrant by pulling the shotgun trigger on that Philadelphia night.

Three weeks later, Tieri sent word to Caponigro that he was wanted in New York City. A call was made to a designated pay phone in Newark, just a few blocks from Tony Bananas' bar, with the summons. Caponigro had anticipated the invitation from the day that his plot to kill Bruno began.

The crowning of a new king was at hand. His right-hand man, Freddie Salerno, had answered the ringing phone.

Genovese boss Chin Gigante was sending a car for Caponigro and Salerno, arriving at 1:00 p.m., to bring the men into the city. The Chin himself would be waiting, along with Tieri. The voice at the other end was abrupt, providing only the bare-bones details. Without waiting for a reply, the man abruptly hung up.

Salerno was offended by the rudeness of the call, making him wonder if the coronation was actually something else. He kept his concerns to himself, convinced that it was nothing more than mob-induced paranoia, and began his walk back to the bar and his boss.

Caponigro waited impatiently for Salerno's return, checking the time on his pricey Piaget watch. The excitement rose within him, as it had each day since the killing, that today was the day Caponigro had waited for his entire life. At 11:30 a.m., Salerno found his boss standing in the doorway of the bar awaiting Salerno's return, the door's handle in his hand as he looked up the Newark street.

From thirty feet away, Salerno flashed a smile and a thumbs-up to Caponigro—now with a look of childlike delight on his weathered face. "Tony, it will be today," the herald announced in an excited voice that belied his concerns about what exactly this day would hold.

But Salerno's worries were entirely his own. Caponigro, blinded by visions of his imminent ascension, thought only about the car coming from New York to pick them up. It couldn't arrive soon enough to suit him. The ensuing ride was all that separated him from the seat atop the Philadelphia Mafia.

Forgotten was the old mob maxim: you cannot kill a boss

unless the entire Commission gives its approval—the key word being *entire*. Caponigro, hearing what he wanted to hear, went forward only on the say-so of the clever Tieri. What was done could not be undone, and the pricey sedan dispatched by the Chin headed west from Greenwich Village toward Newark.

The car arrived five minutes early, with the Chin's trusted bodyguard Vinnie DeMaio dispatched as the Genovese family emissary. Caponigro bounded from the club toward the car, with Salerno respectfully walking a few steps behind. Both were dressed to the nines, two real men of La Cosa Nostra going in style. DeMaio led them to the waiting car.

The passengers expected to head toward Gigante's grubby Greenwich Village clubhouse. But DeMaio explained their destination was instead a Brooklyn waterfront warehouse owned by the family. The Bruno murder had turned up the heat in New York as well as in Philadelphia, he explained. The Chin's Triangle club was now under constant FBI surveillance, and the arrival of anyone connected to the Philly family would immediately stamp them as suspects in the execution. Caponigro nodded his assent at the change in plans.

The Manhattan skyline loomed in the distance as the ride continued in silence. They arrived in Brooklyn within an hour, pulling in front of a gray waterfront building with a stark metal gate. The entrance was flanked by two large thugs. One pressed a red button, and the door slowly cranked open for the car to pull inside. The sedan topped about twenty feet away from a group of men whose faces were indistinguishable in the dim warehouse light. DeMaio and the driver exited, stepping aside into the shadows. As the voice of Tieri echoed through the dank building, the reality of the situation suddenly hit Caponigro—this was the end, not the beginning.

"Tony, come over here," Tieri beckoned. "Vincent is in the rear office. We'll go together."

As Natale heard the tale, Caponigro turned and apologized to his old friend Salerno for putting him in the middle of this disaster. "If I have to go, I couldn't go with a better man," Salerno replied.

Caponigro's body was found on April 18, 1980, in the South Bronx. The treacherous capo's corpse bore mute testimony to the gauntlet of violence that comprised his last moments of life: He was beaten. Strangled. Stabbed. Shot. The corpse, stuffed inside a mortuary body bag, showed signs of torture. There was one other discovery: $300 in $20 bills were found stuffed in his mouth and up his ass.

Salerno's body, in a similarly gruesome state, was found the same day about four miles away with the same cash deposit. He'd taken three bullets behind the right ear, and one more behind the left. Most of the bones in his face were broken, and rope burns were on his neck, wrists, and ankles.

The message was clear: these two men were killed by their own greed.

It took six months to track down Sindone ally John "Johnny Keys" Simone, a cousin of Bruno's whose specific role in the hit is as unclear as the penalty for his part was obvious. The mobster—in hiding since the murder—was lured to his death by the promise that his penalty would be an exile from Philadelphia to his vacation home in sunny Florida. The hit was done by the Gambino family, with Simone's body found in a wooded area of Staten Island. He had two last requests: Simone wanted to be killed by a made man. And he wanted his shoes taken off—Simone had once promised his wife that he would die barefoot. Both requests were honored by future Gambino family underboss Sammy "the Bull" Gravano.

This left only Sindone, who had bolted from Philadelphia for his beachfront condo in California to weather the upcoming storm in the sunshine. He was armed with a bogus ID and some credit cards issued under an alias in case his West Coast stay lasted longer than anticipated. Sindone's whereabouts were known to just one man, his protégé Joseph "Chickie" Ciancaglini. The strapping mob enforcer handled collections for Sindone, but he was now listening to the new boss: Philip Testa. The last plotter proved the most elusive of the targets, even as the hunt for the traitor began within a week of the killing.

Testa, on the advice of his new consigliere, Scarfo, called Ciancaglini to a meeting where the two new family executives planned to squeeze Sindone's pal for information. Ciancaglini knew what was what, and they didn't have to squeeze too hard.

Ciancaglini was taking phone calls from Sindone every other day at a gas station pay phone. The fugitive mafioso was looking for absolution from Testa and was willing to surrender all of the family's loan-sharking business in return for a pass.

Ciancaglini considered his options. Most important, he worried that his ties to Sindone might lead the new regime to suspect his complicity in the killing. The thought rattled in his head as Ciancaglini drove to meet with Testa and Scarfo within a week of the murder. The get-together was set for a South Philly row house belonging to Frank Monte, who ran the family's numbers operation. Nobody lived in the house, which was used as a drop for the day's business.

Ciancaglini knocked with some apprehension before Monte opened the door and led him inside. The forty-five-foot walk from the entrance to the kitchen was the longest of Ciancaglini's life. Scarfo stood for a handshake to welcome their guest, as Natale later heard the tale.

"I'm glad you came so quickly," said Scarfo. "I told Phil that you wouldn't hesitate."

Ciancaglini extended one hand toward Little Nicky. In the other, he held Sindone's lone bargaining chip: two small leatherbound composition books filled with all the details of his now-doomed friend's street money. Testa pulled out a chair for Ciancaglini to take a seat and offered their visitor something to eat. An array of cold cuts, Sicilian bread, and Jersey tomatoes sat on the table before them.

Ciancaglini didn't have much of an appetite. "Phil," he quickly declared, "I had nothing to do with what happened to Ang, on my mother's soul."

Testa offered his hand and a smile, enough to convince Ciancaglini that he would leave the row house on his own two feet rather than inside a rolled-up carpet. "We know," Testa finally replied. "Nicky already sent word to New York that you're in the clear—and that you will help us bring in this motherfucker Sindone for what he allowed those other two motherfuckers to do."

The whole thing had a certain irony. Sindone had agreed to set up the man who'd facilitated his rise through the family. And now Ciancaglini, whose position in the family was the result of his friendship with Sindone, would give up his own benefactor. He turned over the two books—and as a bonus revealed where Sindone stashed his petty cash, which was hardly petty at all.

"This is the true mantra of La Cosa Nostra," Natale

observed ruefully years later, after all his mob illusions were reduced to dust.

When the gas station phone rang the next day, the plan was set in motion. The plotters bided their time until their target was finally swayed, convinced it was safe to come home. Sindone's body, stuffed inside two green plastic trash bags, was found dumped behind a South Philadelphia billiard parlor and supermarket on October 30, 1980. He was shot three times in the head.

While the mob meted out its retribution for the Bruno murder, one of the murderous cabal was already in the wind: John Stanfa. The Sicilian knew his role in the killing was fairly common knowledge. What few others knew was that his uncle John Gambino knew in advance of the mob hit, filled in by Stanfa the mole after Caponigro approached Bruno's driver. Both were in danger of facing the same sentence as the other connivers.

Stanfa reached out to his fellow Zips in New York for a helping hand. Gambino faced a dilemma: he could either kill Stanfa or save his Sicilian kin's ass. He opted for the latter. Stanfa was spirited south to a job in a Maryland pizzeria, his reward for taking down a don now nothing more that kneading dough and working an oven. It took nine months, but the authorities tracked Stanfa down in December—after John Gambino placed an anonymous call to the feds. When asked by FBI agents why he went to New York after the Bruno hit, Stanfa replied in broken English, "To get a cup of coffee. It's a free country, isn't it?"

He was tried and convicted of perjury for lying to a grand jury about his meetings with Sindone and Caponigro. Stanfa was sentenced to six years of federal time, which undoubtedly saved his life. He was now beyond the reach of the mob hierarchy and his own uncle who might embrace a Sicilian-style change of heart toward the backstabbing Stanfa.

The Bruno assassination shook the long-stable family to its core, sending the once rock-solid organization into a long spiral of treachery, incompetence, betrayal, murder, prosecution, and paranoia. Bodies were soon piling up on the South Philly streets and beyond—twenty-four in five years by one count—as four bosses followed Bruno into "the Chair" over the next fifteen years. None could reverse the family's plummeting fortunes, and all wound up dead or behind bars.

18

With Caponigro's claim to the throne dispatched in a brutal fashion, underboss Testa took over as head of the Philadelphia mob. His reign was ended in less than a year by of one of the most notorious hits in the mob's long and bloody history. Natale, from the start, never saw Testa as the right man for the lofty position.

"He looked the part—a fearsome countenance, and he had proven his worth as underboss because of his loyalty to Ang," Natale said. "But his loyalty was not enough to prevent the killing of his boss. When such men are forced by circumstance to take the reins, it is only with good fortune that disasters do not occur."

Phil Testa had exactly twelve months of good fortune ahead of him. And Nicky Scarfo had a lot to do with it when the Chicken Man's luck ran out.

Scarfo's hopes of ever rising under the Bruno regime were nil. The old boss shunted Little Nicky to exile in his own personal Elba of Atlantic City after a series of catastrophes, including the fatal stabbing of a longshoreman over a diner seat at the end of a long, boozy night with Chuckie Merlino. Scarfo became capo of the seagulls and sand.

"The devil," Natale hisses of the Atlantic City gangster. "Pure evil. Boss only by attrition."

Natale never liked or trusted Scarfo, and the feeling was mutual. Ralph went to Bruno with a plan to murder Scarfo, a mission he viewed as a surgeon would the removal of a cancerous organ that threatened the entire body.

"Nicky Scarfo hated me," Natale recalled. " 'Cause he knew I wanted to kill him. He did. Angelo Bruno made me swear to him, face-to-face, that I wouldn't do it. The truth of the matter is he told me, 'No, you can't. His two uncles came over here and helped fight in the old war,' and this and that.

"Why did I want to kill him? Because of what he is. I knew he was in Atlantic City talking to other people. He's gonna cause a problem."

In the early seventies the two men had a run-in over control of Local 54, representing the seaside resort's hotel and restaurant workers. Scarfo had befriended the union's president, Frank Gerace, and tried to lay claim to the labor boss. Natale, backed by the Chicago–New York–Philadelphia triumvirate, was then merging the Atlantic City local with his own, Local 170.

Why? "One reason," Natale explained. "To be in complete control if and when gambling came to Atlantic City."

Scarfo registered a beef over Natale's intrusion into his business and quickly wound up on the losing end of the debate. Angelo Bruno squashed Scarfo's bid for control, firmly ruling that Natale was in complete control of the mob's union interests in Atlantic City. The two unions would eventually become one.

Natale knew that Scarfo was a bitter man with a long memory, and the animosity between the two men lingered. Natale had little use for Scarfo as either a mafioso or a man, as he made clear decades later:

"Nicky Scarfo is a sick, demented man. I'm sorry I listened to Ang, but he made me swear—it was a personal thing. He said it would kill the uncles. I told him, 'Go to Sicily for a couple weeks, go take a trip. Just leave it to me.' And he said, 'You can't do that.'"

With Bruno now gone and Natale locked up, Scarfo's eyes were refocused on the prize—boss of the family, king of Atlantic City. Even on the night when the Commission anointed Testa, the South Jersey mobster worked the room inside the executive suite at the ritzy St. Regis Hotel as if he were one of their peers.

The sight was enough to send a shiver through Testa's soul despite his rise to the lofty spot, succeeding his old friend Bruno. He felt like an outsider among these New York men who were now his equals. Even his outfit, an expensive but simple suit, seemed out of place on this night of nights.

Part of the blame belonged to the late Bruno, who kept Testa close to himself and far away from the mob's hierarchy beyond the Philadelphia city limits. But Testa was cheered by his new consigliere Scarfo's friendship with the New Yorkers, believing his loyal pal's ties would benefit Testa's reign.

And his spirits were boosted by a conversation with Gambino boss Castellano that left both bosses smiling. Big Paul had reminded him of the pact made by their predecessor when it came to looting Atlantic City and its unions.

But it was not Castellano who welcomed Testa to the bosses' ranks, a subtle sign of the shifting alliances already under way. Bobby Manna stood instead, a glass of champagne in his hand as the other bosses sat around a large table, to welcome Testa. "To the new boss of the Philadelphia family, Phil Testa," the Genovese consigliere declared to the clinking of glasses. There were handshakes and hugs of welcome and congratulations, along with a promise of help—if needed—in restoring order to the new Testa family.

The thoughts of Scarfo, from his seat in the same suite, were already drifting to the next morning in Atlantic City. He was also busily compiling a mental hit list, with one name at the top: John McCullough. Natale knew exactly what Scarfo was thinking: "Now that Ang is gone, and Ralphy's buried in Lewisburg, their ends of Atlantic City come directly to us. There's no one left to come to us for what used to be Ralphy's."

Scarfo shared his thoughts with the new boss on their ride home from Manhattan, holding the promise of fast cash from Local 54's health and welfare pension funds as a carrot for Testa. The money was particularly enticing for Testa, whose previous earnings were dependent on his ties to the late Bruno. Scarfo appeared poised to open a spigot flowing with riches.

On the morning after the Commission officially installed Testa, Little Nicky summoned union boss Gerace to his home—an invitation delivered by the terrifying Virgilio. Scarfo appeared in a robe and slippers, while his guest stood as a show of respect to the newly promoted gangster. He sat in the kitchen near the lone window, where an unusually high cinder-block wall blocked the sunshine.

There was a tale behind the wall's construction. Scarfo contracted for its creation over fears that Natale might one day pay an early-morning visit to resolve their feud with a few hollow points, ignoring Bruno's orders to the contrary.

Scarfo offered Gerace a smile that belied the glare in his eyes. He explained that the union now belonged to him and promised a larger cut of the cash to the union head. Gerace, who had a wife, kids, and a mistress to support, saw a vision of the future: No financial worries. His girlfriend, now working in his office, set up in a home of her own, free to work only on her tan and taut physique. A steady stream of cash as the union membership exploded from seven hundred dues-paying members to more than twenty thousand.

Gerace's role was simple: In addition to access to the union money, he would arrange for a consulting firm to find companies that would handle various union duties. The businesses would pay dearly for the access, and the money would come back to the mob.

It sounded too good to be true, mostly because it was. By 1982, *The New York Times* was already reporting Gerace's ties to the Scarfo crew. Subtlety was not among Scarfo's limited charms.

On this March morning in 1980, such concerns were not part of the agenda. Scarfo envisioned the same windfall as Gerace: he would enjoy the ear of Phil Testa, whose knowledge of the free-flowing cash would come only from the lying mouth of his new consigliere.

The future seemed bright, with the promise of fast cash for the family. None of it was going to Natale, one of the architects of the mob's grip on the revitalized seaside resort. It would take only a few short years for Scarfo to undo what was so carefully put in place by the prescient bosses of New York, Chicago and Philadelphia.

Testa "failed to see the obvious, that the foundation of Atlantic City—the union—was now in the hands of his murderous partner, Nicky Scarfo," Natale said in hindsight.

Scarfo's plan had a second part. As Natale knew, this was not a man to let bygones be bygones. The new consigliere was plotting his revenge on all those who'd left him to rot in the wasteland of Atlantic City as they whispered in the Bruno's ear.

"He wanted them to feel what he felt in all those damp, cold years before gambling came to Atlantic City," Natale said. "Before Angelo Bruno was killed."

The Atlantic City of 1980 was a burgeoning mob wonderland when Scarfo invited the new boss for a visit. Little Nicky was behind the wheel as the two men drove to the Resorts International casino—the first of the gambling meccas to rise alongside the Atlantic Ocean. The two men entered the lobby side by side, with Testa marveling at the Carrara marble and plush carpeting. Scarfo's nephew Leonetti walked a respectful step behind the pair.

Slightly ahead waited the hulking Gerace, who lived in mortal fear of the five-foot-five Scarfo. Unlike his predecessor Bruno, the new boss was unused to the position of power that he now held. Bruno was a true peer of the old New York bosses and the Outfit in Chicago. Testa was still feeling his way around. Gerace shook hands with the new don as he looked directly at Scarfo—a small gesture that spoke volumes.

Gerace led the visitors on a tour of the premises. As they walked, Scarfo got down to the business he really wanted to discuss: John McCullough, the popular head of the Roofers Union Local 33. Scarfo broached a subject he had raised before, that another union was nosing around Atlantic City and threatening their stranglehold on the casino business.

He laid out a grim scenario for Testa: McCullough was trying to organize the city's bartenders to form their own union, with their own business agents. They would operate outside Gerace's sphere of influence. No money from this group would find its way west to Philadelphia.

"How the hell did this happen?" Testa asked. Scarfo had a ready answer: McCullough had the backing of his fellow Irishman, the powerful union boss (and old Natale ally) Ed Hanley.

"How the fuck did our friends in Chicago give the green light to Hanley to allow this to happen?" Testa shot back. The explanation was simple: as long as the Outfit got paid each month, they couldn't care less about which union provided the cash. In time, Gerace explained, outsiders could take over Local 54 and turn off the flow of money to Philadelphia.

While initially enraged by the blunt talk, Scarfo soon realized it was to his benefit. McCullough was atop the first wave of interlopers and needed to be stopped right away. He asked for a moment alone with Testa.

"Phil, we can't allow them Irish motherfuckers to take all of this away," said Scarfo, waving his arm toward the jangling slot machines and busy gaming tables. "Too many people have worked at this, it belongs to us. The Philly family needs to show we can police our own territory and protect what is ours."

Testa reacted with emotion, rather than the patience and consideration needed in such a situation. The boss, standing inside the first floor of the casino, approved a contract for

Scarfo to murder McCullough. The decision had repercussions that the new boss could never imagine.

The contract was given to the dapper Martorano, suddenly a part of Scarfo's murderous inner circle after all those years with Bruno as his partner.

Nine days before Christmas 1980, a flower deliveryman knocked on the door of McCullough's home, carrying an armful of holiday poinsettias. McCullough was talking on the phone as his wife stood in the kitchen watching when the visitor dropped the flowers and opened fire. McCullough was shot six times and died right in front of his horrified wife.

"Shameful," Natale said of the killing. "A complete disregard of all La Cosa Nostra rules of killing any man. In front of his family! John McCullough was as courageous and tough a man as ever put on a pair of pants. A Marine, and a World War Two hero."

Nicky Scarfo was just getting started.

19

Shortly after Testa's ascension, he selected a longtime Philly mob figure as his underboss—family capo Pete Casella, a convicted heroin dealer who did seventeen years behind bars without ever opening his mouth, a true stand-up guy from the mob's old guard. Before the appointment became official, Casella visited the stone-front home of Frank "Chickie" Narducci on South Broad Street, where the host's wife, Adeline, poured coffee and offered to make breakfast. Casella politely declined, and the two men began to talk. They had a shared history: Narducci had come to Casella's aid when the mob veteran returned to Philly after doing his drug-rap time.

"Chickie admired him," Natale explained. "Casella was known in the family at one time as the number two hatchet man, right behind Skinny Razor. Chickie told him, 'You come with me.' He set him up on the outside, with new clothes and an apartment."

This meeting was about the present, not the past. Narducci broached the idea of Casella's appointment to the number two spot. Casella replied that job one was taking care of Bruno's killers. Job two was making sure Scarfo didn't get the underboss position.

"I give you my word," Casella declared, "that little snake Scarfo will never be what he thinks he will be. The best he will get is the number three spot. If for any reason this does not come about, then—and only then—you and I will talk again."

The two men hugged as Narducci's nervous wife made the sign of the cross for both of them in another room. Casella's prediction on the new arrangement of the family hierarchy was spot-on.

His promotion was met with approval by the made men of Philadelphia and the bosses of New York. The lone dissenting voice was Scarfo, relegated to the family's number three spot—but he made no public pronouncement of his feelings.

For Natale, the Chicken Man's choices for the top spots provided further evidence of the new boss's chief failure after assuming the seat of power. Casella and Scarfo had little use for one another, creating a schism at the very inception of the new regime.

"It's like he never heard or read the old axiom 'those who don't study history are doomed to repeat it,'" said Natale. "In his haste to appease all the factions of the family, he made a grave mistake in his choices as underboss and consigliere. He failed to recognize the Bruno killing had shattered the aura of invincibility that surrounded the men who rule and set free the demons of unrealistic ambitions and the greed of men who wanted to be more than they were ever born to be."

Testa's biggest fault was putting even an ounce of trust in his friend and consigliere Scarfo: "He was a nonentity until

Angelo Bruno was murdered, and then he fell into the role he was born to play: a sycophant who took advantage of Testa. The face of the Philly mob was transformed from the benevolent profile of Bruno into the face of greed and treachery embodied by Scarfo.

"As Willie Shakespeare would say, 'Therein lies the problem.'"

Testa stood flanked by his two choices for the ruling troika inside the dimly lit basement of a South Philly row house as the family conducted its swearing-in ceremony for its new leaders. The smell of damp mortar mingled with the smoke from burning candles. Testa, looking every inch the rightful successor as padrone, wore a dark gray pin-striped suit.

Through the flickering candlelight, he could make out the face of his son Salvie—there to witness the installation of the new boss, the young man's father. The pride was obvious on both their faces. The ceremony would also include the induction of new members into the family, including the younger Testa. For many, his arrival as a made man marked Salvie's designation as heir apparent.

"Salvie was the prince in waiting," said Natale, who'd known the young Testa since the new inductee was a boy. "He was a gangster's gangster. He had the DNA. Pure. He tasted the power, growing up the way he did. And once you feel that, it's hard to get rid of. It's like heroin. End of story."

Sworn in alongside Salvie were Scarfo's nephew "Crazy Phil" Leonetti, Salvatore "Wayne" Grande, Anthony "Blonde Babe" Pungitore, Chickie Narducci's son Frank, and two others. Salvie and Leonetti invited the new inductees and the rest to join them for an after-party at the Saloon, a bar-restaurant in the oldest and most heavily Italian section of the city.

Pungitore's oldest son, Joe, helped ferry the revelers to their celebration. Salvie Testa was the main attraction, drawing an admiring crowd of male mob wannabes and attractive young women—including Maria Merlino, whose father, Chuckie, would later move into the family's ruling hierarchy.

The men shared a dinner, served promptly at 8:00 p.m., and toasted one another with champagne and iced vodka as the gawkers stared. The very public meeting was meant as a dual statement of purpose: Here we are. And the city belongs to us. Casella, who'd received his button forty years earlier, was the only one to turn down the invitation.

"I love you," the ever-respectful Salvie told his old man at the ceremony, planting a kiss on his cheek. "And I am at your service no matter what."

The preparty event struck Natale years later as among the most ironic gatherings in Philly mob history. All assembled pledged allegiance to the family and the new don, including Casella and Scarfo.

"Here, standing together while swearing a vow of loyalty, were the men who within a few short years would break every promise—including the oath of omertà—to Phil Testa and La Cosa Nostra," Natale said of the ceremony. "Never in the history of the family was a ceremony so ripe with men who would be a part of killing one another."

The first to turn, against all odds, was the veteran Casella.

Among Casella's friends was local hood Rocco Marinucci, who in turn had a pal named Teddy DiPretoro—a waiter at Bookbinder's, a popular seafood restaurant on the Delaware River. The two aspiring gangsters did a bit of drug dealing, and Marinucci was particularly determined to become a made man. DiPretoro boasted a talent for manufacturing silencers, bombs, and assorted other weaponry in his basement.

Casella was soon accompanied everywhere by the young hoodlums as Scarfo connived to omit the underboss from his discussions with Testa and keep the elder mobster in the dark about the Atlantic City money. What Scarfo forgot was that the Philly mob veteran had friends inside the Gambino family, too, men who had done time in Atlanta alongside Casella.

Casella's eyes were opened during a New York social call with his old cellmates. Accompanied by Narducci, Casella checked into the St. Regis Hotel in midtown Manhattan for a weekend reunion in January 1981. Tommy Bilotti, one of boss Castellano's most trusted men, invited the pair to a small Sunday dinner gathering at a tiny Italian restaurant closed to all but the mobsters. Each table was covered by a checkered tablecloth, a sight right out of every mob movie ever made about New York.

Bilotti brought one other guest: a Gambino captain jailed alongside Casella. The man would vouch for both Bilotti and Casella, an old Mafia tradition, since the two had never met. Dinner was served, but this was a business meeting as well.

"Tommy Bilotti was a tough guy," Natale said of Big Paul's right-hand man. "If he had something to say, he said it—no questions asked. Paul Castellano needed someone like him."

Once the formalities were finished, Bilotti congratulated Casella on his promotion to underboss. He also offered his compliments on the windfall that came with the new position, the buckets of cash liberated from the funds of Local 54. It was the first that Casella or Narducci had ever heard about the money that was already coming the way of Testa and Scarfo.

"When he heard the money was supposed to be shared equally, between Castellano, Philly, and Chicago—he wasn't getting a dime!" Natale recounted of the meeting. "He was dumbfounded. Being the man he is, he always played it straight. And that's when he said, 'We gotta do something now.' That's what ignited the whole plot against Phil Testa.

"Casella thought, 'I've gotta get something out of this, even if it's just three cents.' That's the evilness of our life. The greed, with people saying, 'Eh, that guy, he don't need this, he don't need that.'"

Casella made it through the meal before excusing himself, mentioning a meeting scheduled that night in Philadelphia with Testa. The two old gangsters shared an embrace, with Bilotti sending along greetings to both the new boss and his son, Salvie. Bilotti had earlier shared his private number with Casella, and he urged the Philly made man to use it—particularly if there was any trouble with Scarfo.

"Keep your eyes and ears open for anything," Bilotti said in parting. "These are dangerous times for the Philadelphia family after a man like Angelo Bruno was murdered by his own."

Casella was reeling as he walked outside the restaurant under the gray city sky. The two Philly vets climbed into their car for the ride home, with Narducci at the wheel. "Not now," Casella said with a wave of his hand, calling for silence as they drove through the crowded Manhattan streets. But both men were considering the treachery exposed over dinner. And they both believed something had to be done about this disrespectful slap in the face.

"So be it," Casella finally said, more to himself than Narducci, and let out a sigh. This was Pete Casella's pinpoint in time, riding along the turnpike back to his hometown. Two-thirds of the family's ruling triumvirate had treated him like a fool, hoarding the income from Atlantic City for themselves. The sting of this realization soon evolved into anger and vengeance before Casella finally shared his thoughts with Narducci:

"Chickie, when we enter Philly, we go into town as when we left, knowing nothing about Atlantic City and what we were told. Then we call Rocco and tell him to bring the kid who's the expert with the guns and bombs."

Narducci turned to look at his friend: "Can I say something now? I've never been happier than at this moment." The exchange marked the beginning of the end for Testa, barely ten months into his reign as boss. To the men driving south, Phil Testa was already a dead man walking.

Narducci wasn't done. He wanted to take out Scarfo as well and proposed that he personally pump two bullets into Little Nicky's head. Casella remained focused on Testa, knowing that the New York bosses would be outraged by a second unsanctioned Philly killing so close to the murder of Bruno.

A plot soon evolved: They would make the mob hit appear as payback for the murder of union boss McCullough, which was backed by Testa. Casella and Narducci were actually sharing dinner on the night of the McCullough murder, with news of the assassination personally delivered to their table by the restaurant's owner.

McCullough's friends in the union and his allies in the Irish Republican Army would shoulder the blame. Because the IRA was famously proficient with bombs, they would detonate an explosive device and blow Testa to kingdom come.

DiPretoro and Marinucci met with the underboss and Narducci in the Villa di Roma, a restaurant in the heart of the Italian Market. The traitorous quartet made their plans and pledged their mutual allegiance. The sands were now running quickly from the hourglass of Testa's life.

The murder weapon would be a keg filled with roofers' nails placed atop sticks of dynamite. DiPretoro would design the simple bomb using twenty sticks of dynamite, and Marinucci would hit the detonator. On March 15, 1981—six days short of the first anniversary of Bruno's demise—the two men sat inside a van parked near Testa's upscale home.

At 2:55 a.m., the Chicken Man walked toward the front door after double-parking his 1980 Chevrolet Caprice Classic on the street. A massive explosion tore suddenly through the night, a blast so powerful that the porch was torn to pieces and debris scattered for fifty feet across the property. The front door was blown thirty feet into the kitchen, with an eight-foot-wide hole torn in the front façade of the house.

Testa was pronounced dead a short time later at St. Agnes Hospital. The cops found $10,000 cash in his pockets. "He looked like he went through a giant paper shredder," said one eyewitness. The bomb plot had worked, too; media reports soon suggested the killers were friends of McCullough's exacting their revenge.

Natale was less surprised by the second murder of a Philadelphia boss in just under a year. "Pure La Cosa Nostra, finding a reason to justify killing a onetime friend," he reflected. "Although in this case it was not hard, considering the treachery involved with Atlantic City."

When law enforcement searched Testa's home, they found a VCR and just two tapes: *The Godfather,* parts one and two.

As he had one year earlier after the Bruno murder, Scarfo called his old prison pal Manna from the Genovese family. This time, he was plotting to fill the suddenly vacant seat as head of the volatile Philly family, where decades of peace were forgotten after this second brutal execution. This time, the killers were Pete Casella and Chickie Narducci, Scarfo told his friend.

Only days later, Scarfo's nephew Phil Leonetti was standing alongside an Atlantic City pay phone inside an Italian restaurant at 6:00 p.m.—the designated number for the Genovese family to hear from Little Nicky. Leonetti had driven a few short blocks to the location, insuring no one could lob a shot at him on the streets. The call was short and the message terse: Leonetti was wanted at 10:00 a.m. the next day in Manhattan. Make sure nobody is following you.

Click.

Leonetti arrived thirty minutes early, with a burly doorman leading him inside a luxurious condo on the Upper East Side. His uncle had briefed Leonetti the night before, and the young gangster took the elevator to the fourth floor, where he was greeted by Manna's muscle—two men the size of Mack trucks. A third man greeted him by name and led Leonetti inside, where Manna awaited.

The apartment was redolent of Italian coffee and Cuban cigars. Leonetti entered and kissed his host on both cheeks. Casella might somehow have reached the Genovese family before Scarfo, but the die was already cast. All the fears were dispersed as Manna began to speak, his message as clear as the church bells ringing on a Sunday morning back in South Philly.

Manna offered his condolences for the killing of Testa. The Genovese family was on board with Scarfo's version of what happened, and so was the entire Commission—now fully under the sway of the Chin's powerhouse family.

The Philadelphia branch was placeo in the hands of a murderous psychopath: Little Nicky Scarfo. Blood would flow and the family soon flailed.

"Bobby Manna set loose what Scarfo had kept dormant in the darkest part of his soul," Natale mused years later. "The bitterness of those years when he was regarded by Angelo Bruno and his fellow made men as unstable in his dealings with other men. Manna based his opinions on the years when they walked the yard in New Jersey, where Scarfo hid his devious nature behind a verbiage of flattery that distracted Bobby from digging any deeper."

Natale recalled a time when Scarfo's stock was so low that the city's top drug dealers spurned his company and turned up their noses when he called to distribute their product and line his pockets. Now, Scarfo decreed, they would pay his family tribute—or face the lethal consequences. Any drug dealers who balked would face a death sentence, with no appeal.

"He unleashed a bloodbath without reason or direction," said Natale. "He did this for only one purpose, to instill fear in the hearts of enemies created only by his own paranoia. And also in the minds of his own newly baptized soldiers."

Scarfo made one other move: he brought Bruno's old partner Martorano into the family as a made man. The Docile Don had refused his friend's requests for two decades. But in April 1981, Martorano received his button along with Salvatore "Shotsie" Sparacio. Martorano, as a meth maker himself, knew all the other major players in the drug game and shared his wealth of industry knowledge with the new boss.

Martorano also agreed, within a month, to serve up two of his best friends from their mutual business, Harry Peetros and Stevie Bouras, members of the city's so-called Greek Mob—an affiliation of about a dozen that also dealt in gambling and loan-sharking.

"Long John became a made man on the bodies of his friends," recounted Natale with disdain. "And he never even pulled the trigger."

Peetros and Long John were business partners and friends, often dining together—Martorano with his wife, and the Greek with his girlfriend du jour.

Martorano had broached the idea of partnering with Scarfo to Peetros, who brushed aside the suggestion as the two shared what became their final meal, with an appetizer of beluga caviar and champagne, at a five-star restaurant.

"You've got to be kidding," said Peetros. "I'll gladly send him an envelope every month out of respect, but I've put my balls on the line all of my life. And now he wants to emasculate me."

Martorano appeared confused until Peetros gave him the definition of *emasculate*—"He wants to take my manhood away from me." The two men excused themselves from the table to continue their conversation, with Martorano lending a sympathetic ear to his old pal.

"Harry, I'll fix this," he said confidently. "The monthly thing will be enough. Let's go over and join our ladies." Once seated, Long John reached into an ice bucket to remove a chilled bottle of vodka. He poured the booze into a pair of snifters and raised his glass in a toast: "To tonight, and forever our friendship."

Peetros, who usually picked up the tab for their nights on the town, was only the first to die. Two nights after their dinner, his body was found inside the trunk of his gold Cadillac on May 25, 1981. His last ride ended when the luxury car was parked on a quiet street about a mile outside the city limits. He died secure with Martorano's assurance that his decision to stiff Scarfo would come without consequence.

Natale said Peetros's mistake was a failure to gauge the sudden change in Scarfo's mob stature, along with the everlasting enmity of Little Nicky toward those who had once looked down their noses at him. And Peetros completely misjudged Martorano's relationship with the new boss.

"He made a brave mistake because Long John was in deadly fear of this miniature gangster," said Natale.

The Peetros killing came with a maniacal twist: Martorano arranged for Bouras, his next target, to pull the trigger. Bouras, kingpin of a multimillion-dollar methamphetamine ring, was recruited by a promise from Long John that the execution would insure his independence from the Scarfo regime, along with control of Peetros's drug business.

Martorano played his business partner like a Stradivarius in what Natale called "The Mafia Triangle." He explained the double-dealing this way: "When there are two men who have the same friend, and they both trust him, it was simple—use one to kill the other. The reason? Survival."

Bouras received a call for a dinner date two days later from Martorano. Long John was bringing his wife, and he arranged a dinner companion for Bouras. Knowing of Bouras's interest in an attractive South Philly woman named Jeanette Curro, an invite was extended to her as well. On its face, the dinner appeared a nod of congratulations on a job well done in the Peetros hit.

Like so many other things in the world of La Cosa Nostra, the truth proved far more sinister.

The couples, joined by some other guests, assembled at the Meletis restaurant on May 27—a beautiful spring day, with temperatures in the low seventies. Martorano found his killer for this hit much closer to home: his troubled son, George.

Natale recalled that George, known as Cowboy, struggled as a kid with an attention deficit disorder and relied on medication to control his condition. The son had never killed a man in his life. But his greedy father was more focused on his future in the crime family than worried about his own kin.

As Natale heard the tale, Bouras—a seasoned killer possessed of the sixth sense needed to survive in his treacherous business—was oblivious of the warning signs of impending doom as he turned all his attention toward Curro. He never noticed when Martorano arranged the seating so that Bouras was closest to the restaurant's entrance. Bouras never saw the two men enter the restaurant through that front door until it was too late. Both shooters wore their winter clothes despite the warm weather: one in a ski mask and a long coat, the other with a wool scarf wrapped around his face.

"Ah, c'mon now, fellas," said Bouras when he saw the pair marching toward the table. Those were his final words. The younger Martorano and his dad's bodyguard started firing indiscriminately from ten feet away, with the inexperienced Georgie emptying his weapon. The pair didn't stop shooting until Bouras was dead. Killed alongside the meth dealer was his innocent date, Jeanette Curro.

Natale, though no stranger to the murderous ways of the mob, was repulsed when he heard the story: "A scene from hell. The father has his son kill a man in front of his mother? As simple as asking him to run an errand, asking him to lose his immortal soul for the aspirations of the father to find a top position in the Philly family."

20

When Ralph arrived at Lewisburg, facing another quarter century away from his hometown and the Philly mob, the dire circumstances of his life finally hit the gangster. Angelo Bruno was dead and gone, and so was the money once sent to Natale's family. His future appeared as dreary as the nondescript surroundings.

"You see them gray walls, you see them gun towers," he recalled. "And you got a long sentence, and you say, 'Look where I gotta do this time—in the middle of Pennsylvania!'"

Oddly enough, he was struck by perhaps the lone bit of fatherly advice that Spike Natale had ever offered him. The old man, after sizing up his young son, saw a long prison stretch somewhere in the boy's adult future.

"My father didn't tell me too many things, but he told me this," Natale said before repeating the words verbatim.

"I know you're going away for a long time at some point," Spike lectured him. "Remember one thing when it happens. It may sound harsh now, but remember this. You have to forget everything and everybody—your wife, your kids, your girl.

Everything! Because if you don't, you'll think about that every day, and when you come home, you'll be half a man. And they can't do that to you."

Another bit of prison counsel came from the facility's African-American inmates. "As my black brothers use to tell their black brothers when they came in, 'It's too late to get scared now,'" Natale said.

One visitors' day early on, his brother Michael arrived at the correctional facility with their mom. The two came through the front gate, enduring a weapons check on the way inside. This was a strange, alternate reality for solid-citizen Michael—a successful musician, the lead trumpet player for Philly talk show host Mike Douglas's band, and a professor at Temple University. Ralph used to tease his straight-arrow sibling that they came from different parents.

"Mom, are you sure?" he asked with Michael in listening range. "Me and him?"

This time, a stunned Michael did the talking after sitting down with Ralph inside the drab Lewisburg visiting room: "How can you do it? How can you stay here?"

Ralph's answer came back terse and true: "Michael, I have no choice. I gotta stay here."

Before Michael could answer, their mother spoke to her imprisoned son in a voice heavy with disdain. "Ralph, look at you."

But Natale cut her off before she could utter another syllable. "Mom, I gotta tell you something before we get into this. I'm glad you made me what I am. You made me tough. I don't care what they do to me. I gotta tell you that right to your face."

When Michael left with their mother, he threw up outside the prison walls and never returned. "And I can understand that," Natale said. "I don't know if I ever got used to it, but it didn't bother me after a while. That's frightening."

The high school dropout became a reader behind bars, everything from reference books to Ernest Hemingway's classic novels. "When I had nothing to do, I would read the dictionary—from the front to the back, from the back to the front. In jail, you got nothing to do. And if you're doing real time, you don't have a TV in your room—all you got is a cell. So I read incessantly. And I thought about things."

He also became a regular at the weekly Sunday masses behind the prison walls. "Billy DiPasquale, the brother of 'Mad Dog' DiPasquale, he was the altar boy. But everyone was serious about it. We went to church. Nobody would dare sneer at you, because a lot of good men went every Sunday. It was terrible to see such a nice man like the priest, a great guy, inside that prison."

On one memorable occasion, the stone killer became a man of peace, brokering a deal between the prison's Black Mafia and the prison administration. Complaints over living conditions led to a hunger strike by the African-Americans, including a few doing life for the murders of seven people inside a Washington, DC, home owned by future NBA Hall of Famer Kareem Abdul-Jabbar.

Natale sat down with the inmates, then approached the prison guards.

"I just said, 'If you'll do this and that, the strike will be over,'" Natale recalled nonchalantly. "And they did, and the strike ended. Whenever the Black Mafia had a beef after that, they came to me. And they remembered that."

No matter his other prison pursuits, Natale remained obsessed with avenging Bruno and taking control of the

Philadelphia family. "That was my quest. To take back Philadelphia from whoever was in charge. And to take back what
once belonged to me and Angelo Bruno." The scenario was
never far from his thoughts.

By 1982, the cash crunch created in the Natale household
by Ralph's imprisonment was real and getting worse. Natale
kept waiting for his old mob cohorts to do right by his family,
but not a penny found its way to Lucia or the kids. When
she came to visit Ralph, the two shared a fiscal summit to
face the new realities.

"I told her, 'We'll be okay. Sell the house. Sell the one in
Palm Springs, too. And make sure the kids have enough to
go to school,'" Natale remembered. "You know what my
wife did? She's a queen. She started cleaning other people's
apartments, certain people that she liked. She cooked for
them a little bit. She cleaned other people's toilets, and still
I wouldn't become a rat. She took care of herself and sent
me commissary money.

"Imagine that! I could cry when I think of it. But she
did it."

His daughters, their father in prison, worked their way
through school as waitresses. Natale, alone in his cell at night,
asked for divine intervention to help him make it through:
"I prayed to the Blessed Mother. I figured she's gonna help
me out. Help my family out. Look, the things I did in my
life and I was still alive—there musta been somebody really
cared for me."

21

MR. NATALE GOES TO WASHINGTON

In early 1982, Natale found himself in front of a federal parole board for a review of his sentence. The three-member group seemed perplexed: Why was he doing twenty-seven years when the federal sentencing guidelines called for fifty-two to eighty months—just under seven years?

"They talked it over, and they said, 'We're gonna recommend a reduction. We're not gonna set you free, but you can't do twenty-seven years,'" recalled Natale. "Maybe I woulda done eight, nine, I woulda been home."

The elated Natale thanked them profusely, shook everyone's hand, and was told to expect word in a month. He called Lucia with the good news, and she came up to visit with the wives of fellow Mafia members Ronnie Turchi and George Flynn. They arrived in the visitors' area, with three guards watching every move on the floor below—and then Mrs. Natale's visit was interrupted by one of the corrections officers. Her husband was needed in the warden's office when they were finished.

The couple said good-bye and Natale headed to see the

warden, with no idea of the group assembled waiting for his presence.

"Six, seven, eight suits are there!" he remembered. "From Washington—they told me about a Senate investigating committee. They told me, 'If your answers are correct, and we know you're not a liar'—all that bullshit—'we will recommend a reduction, and you could be home in maybe three or four months.'"

The response, as it had in Florida, came instantly to Natale's lips: "I'm afraid you got the wrong guy. Can I go back to my cell?" The parole folks had already offered him what was now on the table from the feds.

Natale was in the prison's Red Top, the red-tiled center area of Lewisburg, when his counselor summoned him for another meeting. He couldn't imagine what the problem was—an argument with another inmate? His mind began racing—with a sentence reduction awaiting, Natale was keenly aware of keeping his nose clean.

An envelope was waiting from the Senate committee. The counselor said he had no idea what was inside. Natale, on the other hand, knew what was waiting.

"They put the carrot in front of me with the parole, and then I go up there to the warden's office," he said ruefully. "And when I don't speak, a week after that, I heard that I've been denied by the parole board for my reduction. It's unheard of. But it happened."

So did the trip to testify before the Senate committee. On June 22, 1982, Mr. Natale went to Washington, arriving with a grant of immunity from the panel waiting to question him. It would become a life-defining moment, when all of the lessons learned across the decades from Skinny Razor and Angelo Bruno were put to the ultimate test.

He was brought directly from solitary confinement at Lewisburg to the Dirksen Senate Office Building in Washington. Lucia took the Amtrak train south from Jersey with their daughters Rebecca and Carmen for their first opportunity to see Ralph outside a federal prison in three years. The trio jumped in a cab for the last leg of their journey.

The public hearing on organized crime was a big deal, with the Senate committee looking to hang some prize heads on the office wall before a media horde. Their targets: Chicago boss Anthony Accardo, Natale's old Philadelphia nemesis Nicky Scarfo, and longtime union pal Ed Hanley. The panel wanted Natale's long-held secrets about Atlantic City and the deal hatched in Ferraro's over coffee and dessert.

Ralph knew his words held the keys to any hopes of imminent freedom. He also knew they would be chosen carefully and reveal little, no matter the cost to himself—or his wife or his kids. He felt a tinge of pride, too, since the federal invitation certified that Senate investigators were aware of his pivotal role in the nexus of organized crime and organized labor.

"You gotta remember, I'm jammed up," he says now. "Imagine that—that Atlantic City money is there. I put that together with Angelo, Carlo Gambino, and Tony Accardo. And not a dime of it was going to my family."

A look of pure disgust covers his face as he spits out two names: "Nicky Scarfo. Phil Testa."

The captain assigned to guard the summoned witness showed some sympathy for Natale's plight, directing him to a bathroom with a shower inside the office. "I don't need a shower," Natale told his benefactor. "I just want to wash my face and shave."

Once Natale had cleaned up, the captain allowed Lucia

inside as the two girls—outside in the hallway—peered
through a crack in the office door at their dad. Once they
left, Natale donned his attire for the hearing: dark sports coat,
plain dark tie, white shirt, and slacks, with hair cropped short.
He was freshly shaved and sported an unlikely tan from his
time in the yard. He was accompanied by an attorney, Glenn
Zeitz. Rebecca watched from the hallway, looking at her dad
through a door left ajar.

Natale looked more like the head of a Fortune 500 company than a Mafia cohort jailed for arson and drug dealing
as Senator William Roth of Delaware commenced with the
questioning. Natale's reply, never in doubt as he waited to
take his seat before the panel, was delivered implacably.

"Senator, on the advice of my counsel, I can't answer,"
he said evenly.

Another question.

"I will not answer at this time."

Senator Warren Rudman exploded angrily when Natale
declined to answer a question about providing guns for
Angelo Bruno—and Zeitz intervened.

"You're not here to make speeches to this committee!"
Rudman snapped. "You're here to advise your client. You talk
to Mr. Natale. I'd like him to answer it. He's been instructed
to answer it."

Natale's reply was succinct: "I refuse to answer, Senator."

"Do you understand that you have been instructed to
answer this question?" shot back Roth.

"Yes, I do Senator." Natale had his hands crossed on the
table in front of him.

Roth raised the ante: "Do you understand that in view
of your refusal to testify . . . in response to this subcom-
mittee's grant of immunity, that I believe the record would

support a finding of either civil or criminal contempt on your part? Such a finding could subject you to additional incarceration. I must advise you that such action on your part will not be taken lightly."

The Ralphy of South Philadelphia was suddenly present at the table with his attorney as a bristling Natale responded, "I don't take it lightly either, Senator. I think this panel has went beyond the scope of this investigation, to answer Senator Rudman. You've heard Charlie Allen—he is a complete liar. He tells twenty percent truth and eighty percent lies. I've got twenty-seven years already. They're trying to give me more time on the same case.

"I didn't come in here looking for any extra time. But on something like that, I think it is a trap for me. I wanted to answer the best I could. Right now, I can't beyond that there."

Roth pressed on: Didn't he meet with Bruno on regularly, usually for lunch?

"Yes, I did. He's my friend," Natale replied, referring to his slain boss in the present tense. "He's my friend. Maybe twice a week."

"Did Mr. Bruno give you orders on union matters during these luncheons?" Roth continued.

"Never. Never. I'll take a polygraph for that. See if Charlie Allen will take the same polygraph with me on these questions. Senator, none whatsoever."

Was Angelo Bruno a crime figure?

"He was a fond, adorable man," Natale said evenly. "No, I never heard of those things."

The questions shifted to Ed Hanley. Did they ever meet?

"Many times," said Natale. "He was my boss. He signed my paychecks."

And loans made from union pension funds?

"I'll take a polygraph on all of that also," Natale said combatively.

He was then asked about one of the witnesses to follow, the current boss of the Philadelphia mob—Little Nicky Scarfo. Natale despised Scarfo with every bone in his body. Butter would not melt in his mouth as he answered the questions. But the bitter taste of his responses would never disappear.

"I think Nicky was a bartender at one time," said Natale. "A few years ago in Atlantic City, he was tending bar—I think at the 500 Club. I've known Nicky casually during the last ten, twelve years. That's what I know of him. . . . Nicky's a fine little guy."

And was Scarfo mobbed up?

"No. We were all born and raised there. We don't talk that way about each other."

The grand finale followed, with Rudman and Natale going toe-to-toe like a pair of fighters battling for the championship belt.

"I just want to nail this down, Mr. Natale," the senator jabbed. "In all the years that you were involved in this business, which by anybody's rules is a kind of tough business—you wouldn't deny that, would you?"

"It certainly is," parried the mobster.

"I'm glad we can agreed on that."

Then Natale unloaded a roundhouse: "I'm fighting for my life here. That's why I have to watch what I agree with you on. You have to take that into consideration. I'm not trying to give you a hard time here."

Rudman fired back, "In all those years, you want your testimony before this committee to be that you didn't even know anything about the fact that people like Nicky and Angelo were involved in organized crime?"

"Only what I read in the great, free press."

"Which you didn't believe?"

"Of course not," said the unflappable Natale. "I don't think you believe everything you read in the paper, too, Senator."

Natale did address the claims by witness Charlie Allen that he spent ten years as Ralphy's bodyguard: "What did he do for me? He put me in jail. He never worked for me."

Natale never ceded an inch before security finally shuffled him out of the hearing room and back to the captain's office. The officer knew what the senators wanted from Natale, and he knew the Philadelphia mobster had refused to give it to them.

In grudging admiration, he offered Natale a firm handshake. "Jesus Christ, they don't make 'em like you anymore."

"Thanks. I'm just starting a long bid."

"Yeah. I'm sure you're gonna be fine."

Which wasn't remotely true at this point. Natale's shot at early release was torpedoed. His family would return to their home without him, or much hope of seeing him free anytime soon. His cell at Lewisburg awaited. Yet Natale returned to prison with no regrets.

"I coulda gave them New York, Chicago, Philadelphia." He shrugs. "I did my time—sixteen straight bananas on that one. It just shows you, if I wanted to—but I didn't. It wasn't gonna work for me."

Natale wasn't the only witness called to Washington. Scarfo was subpoenaed and arrived with a small entourage that included a nascent Philadelphia mobster named Joey Merlino. The latter's path would cross with Natale's again, to interesting results, seventeen years down the road in a far different federal venue.

Another summons to our nation's capital came a year later. If the first visit was part of a dog and pony show, the encore was done with far less fanfare. The feds still held out hope of leveraging Natale into a cooperation deal, dangling early release yet again.

Nothing changed.

"They gave me immunity for everything I ever done," Natale recalled of his next go-round. "And they did it in a closed room, not for the public. Nobody. It was still the same answer."

22

A MAFIA PRINCE

The brutal murder of his father unleashed something savage in Salvie Testa, the mob prince with an unlikely past and an uncertain future. The boss's son had shown signs of a bright future in La Cosa Nostra while growing up, and his fearsome reputation would land him on the front of *The Wall Street Journal*—where he was described as "the mob's most celebrated figure these days."

Natale was not surprised by his ascension. "I loved Salvie. I seen him grow up," he said years later with respect. "He kind of admired me from afar. Madonn', he was a killer's killer. No life was killed without reason or sanity."

But his short and criminal life's work was hardly preordained. His father initially steered his son away from the Life, and Salvie attended private Catholic schools—graduating from Saint John Neumann High School. The young Testa attended Philly's Temple University for a year before taking a job as a real estate salesman, working for Bruno's son-in-law. His boss recalled the handsome, athletic six-footer as hardworking, conscientious, gentle, and kind. But like the fictional Michael Corleone, the young man found himself inexorably drawn into his father's orbit.

Natale was walking with Lucia and one of their daughters to visit a South Philly pediatrician when they ran into young Testa shortly before Natale's 1979 arson arrest and incarceration,

"He was walking across the street and he saw us," Natale recounted of his final meeting with Salvie. "He shouts over—'Ralphy!'—and he came over to shake my hand. We talked, and he told me, 'My family wants me to go to college and all that. I don't wanna do that. I wanna do what you do.'

"The mother and father were behind that, going to a good school. But when Phil saw what his son was—Phil wasn't stupid in that regard. Salvie was a real man, and a real gangster."

The first evidence of Salvie's lethal acumen had occurred earlier that year, shortly after Philadelphia rang in the New Year. The second-generation mafioso made his bones on January 4, 1979, whacking a drug dealer named Michael "Mikey Coco" Cifelli inside a South Philly bar. The murder was sanctioned by Bruno and assigned to Scarfo, who selected young Testa and Chuckie Merlino to handle the hit at Priori's on the corner of Tenth and Wolf.

Cifelli's open dealing of methamphetamine was a slap in the faces of Bruno's neighborhood constituents, and the boss acted quickly to remove this scourge from their streets. When Cifelli ignored a friendly suggestion to take his business elsewhere, a lethal Plan B was unleashed.

"Legends, like rivers, must begin at their source," Natale said of the killing. "And Priori's was the beginning of Salvie

Testa. His true nature surfaced, from the core of his being. Even Merlino, who knew him since Salvie was a little boy, couldn't recognize the man now standing in front of him."

The two killers donned ski masks and walked toward Cifelli, who was jabbering on the bar's pay phone. The shooters knew when the call would come; Chuckie had suggested to a mutual friend that he should call Mikey Coco at this exact time to warn him about the contract on his life. Instead of deliverance, the call brought only death.

"This is for you," announced Testa before firing point-blank into his target's skull. Cifelli fell silently to the floor, killed so quickly that he had no time to utter a word of protest or a scream of horror.

Scarfo drove the getaway car. As Natale heard the tale, Testa walked out of the bar and away from his first killing with the gait of a man casually headed to meet an old friend. The howls of terrified patrons echoed in the winter air behind him. Testa climbed into the shotgun seat alongside Little Nicky.

"Did you put two in his head?" asked Scarfo.

"Without a doubt," replied the younger, taller, and better-looking shooter, with panache in his answer. Word of his cavalier approach to killing became the talk of the neighborhood, where Salvie Testa received instant respect as the local mob's Rookie of the Year.

Things changed after the assassination of Bruno and the rise of Philip Testa to boss. Shortly before his own brutal death, the Chicken Man arranged for Salvie's induction as a made man. Around the same time, Testa's wife passed away. With the hit on his father, the young Testa was an orphan at age twenty-five.

"His mother died of cancer," Natale said of the unparalleled mob scion. "That hurt him. And then to see his father get killed like that? He loved his father. And that's what made him what he was. A pure killer."

The mob execution of Phil Testa "took away any chance of Salvie leading a life of any kind of normalcy," Natale said. "His destiny now was to be 'Salvie Testa, the coldest of all the killers' who would rise under Nicky Scarfo."

Natale recalled the tale of Salvie's actions on the day of his father's burial, a cold and windy March morning that felt more winter than spring. As the mourners slowly dispersed, young Testa stood in the cemetery among a small group of boyhood friends offering their support to their precocious leader. He stood among them, not a single tear visible. His stony public face was in contrast to the anguish that Testa felt leaving the hospital emergency room on the night of his father's murder.

Testa asked for a few minutes of solitude as he stood by the graves of his parents, ordering the lingering mourners to wait for him by the cemetery entrance. His mother and father were now together forever, and he stood all alone amid the tombstones.

Phil Testa's casket had not yet gone into the ground, and his son stood for an hour with one arm extended, touching the coffin. His facial expression was now hard, a metamorphosis "into what he was destined to be," said Natale. "The most prolific killer that South Philly had seen since the death of Skinny Razor."

Salvie finally knelt alongside the casket to deliver a solemn vow: "Daddy, I will kill and punish everyone involved with putting you here." He touched the dirt beneath his knees. "I promised I will put such fear into their hearts that even their dogs will forget how to bark."

His initial instinct was to whack everyone outside his father's inner circle. But his upbringing left Salvie acutely aware of the mob's protocols in such matters, and he was persuaded by new boss Scarfo to wait until the Commission gave their approval. The New York families first installed Scarfo as the city's third boss in thirteen months before getting down to the Testa killing. Old pal Manna vouched for Scarfo before the other families as the choice of the Genovese borgata, with Little Nicky installed without opposition. Then Manna laid out the case for Casella as the main force behind this latest bit of mob treachery.

The verdict from New York and the family headed by Gigante was again brutal and brief: kill them all—except Casella, who was given a pass by the Chin, banished to Florida under a threat of immediate execution if he ever reappeared. The worst bloodletting in the often-gory history of the Philadelphia mob was about to commence with the approval of New York, under the shaky hand of Scarfo.

"Nicky Scarfo," Natale said with derision. "Boss by attrition. The darkness of treachery was about to descend over the Philly La Cosa Nostra. There was no one for Nicky to answer to except the face in the mirror when Scarfo shaved."

Then, and only then, did the Testa kid go about avenging the death of his father in spectacular fashion.

On January 7, 1982, Narducci parked his Cadillac about a half block from his home in South Philly. A familiar voice called through the darkness: "Hey, Frank." He turned to see Salvie Testa standing a few feet away, a gun in his hand and malice on his face. The mob prince made sure Narducci had a good look at his executioner before pulling the trigger—again and again and again.

"This is for my father," said Testa before he and sidekick Joe Pungitore emptied their guns into the hapless Narducci, leaving his bullet-riddled body in the street.

"Kills him right on the street, leaves his body on the curb," recalled Natale with admiration. "Boom! Pop-pop-pop. What this kid did was unreal. Chickie Narducci was a capo. Salvie had Pungitore follow him at a distance for days, see what time he would come home, where he would go, what streets he would use. 'Cause Salvie always said, 'I'm gonna kill him.'"

But the killing did little to calm the storm raging inside Salvie Testa, as fellow mobster and future informant Nicholas "Nicky the Crow" Caramandi later recalled while in the embrace of the FBI.

"Salvie used to say to me, 'I wish that motherfucker was alive so I could kill him again.' This is how much he hated this man," the Crow said. "He had no mercy on anybody. Business was business, and killing to him was business."

More was to come. Shortly before the first anniversary of Phil Testa's execution, Salvie had a mutual acquaintance summon Marinucci to a meeting at the Buckeye Club. The unsuspecting second-story man arrived to find a murderous Salvie Testa waiting like a frothing pit bull.

Testa would kill Marinucci, but only after torturing the mob killer until he gave up another name: Teddy DiPretoro, the turncoat who hid the bomb on Salvie's father's front porch.

Marinucci, thirty, was found dead on the first anniversary of the mob hit, his body stuffed inside a green plastic garbage bag and dumped in a South Philly parking lot. It was murder with a message: his mouth was stuffed full with three unexploded firecrackers, a reference to the explosion of March 1981. His hands were tied with clothesline, and he was shot in the chest, neck, and mouth.

DiPretoro was so terrified by word of the execution that he turned himself in to police and began singing like a mob version of Philly's own Teddy Pendergrass. He even confessed to the bizarre May 1980 murder of Edward Bianculli, executed for stealing a box of Valentine's Day candy from a store where DiPretoro worked.

"He thought he was gonna get off on this Testa thing, and then he said, 'I killed this kid,'" recounted Natale. The conspirator turned informant dodged Salvie's payback only by taking a life sentence for both killings.

Salvie Testa's fearsome reputation was burnished by a bizarre ability to dodge death. Three attempts were made on his life as part of a mob war that left two dozen bodies scattered around the Philadelphia area. In 1980, he was shot in the groin and the leg after an angry confrontation outside a local restaurant.

Officials said the shooting was not mob related. The next one most definitely was.

On July 31, 1982, Testa was sitting outside a row house near the Italian Market when a car carrying a killer drove past. The shotgun blast left Testa in critical condition with buckshot wounds to the abdomen, arms, and legs. Just five months later, Testa walked away from a botched hit and gunfight in Washington Square West.

Testa, in contrast with his failed assassins, was so fearsome that he didn't need a gun to take a life. The young mobster and several members of his crew stationed themselves outside a jewelry store run by the relative of a mobbed-up rival. Testa occasionally tapped on the window, an added touch of menace. The man closed up shop on the afternoon of December 14, 1983, marched into his business's walk-in safe, and put a bullet into his head.

The legend of Salvie Testa grew. "I don't have to 'hit' anybody," he boasted. "I just have to tell them I want to talk to them, and they'll do the job for me."

Testa emerged as the cream of an increasingly meager crop of Philly mobsters, preordained in the blood of his father to assume the family mantle of boss. He stepped hard on a few toes along the way. He had a public breakup with his fiancée, Maria Merlino, the daughter of underboss Salvatore "Chuckie" Merlino, only weeks before a wedding viewed as a union of Mafia royalty.

The elder Testa had counseled his son about such affairs of the heart: "Be careful what you say and do with the daughters of my friends." But the young couple had grown up together in the same neighborhood, inescapably brought together at the endless series of baptisms, weddings, and wakes that completed the local circle of life. Their families vacationed together in Margate, on the Jersey shore south of Atlantic City.

The two became romantically involved a year before Phil Testa replaced Bruno as boss.

Testa also had a much-ballyhooed falling out with Scarfo, fueled by rumors started by the infuriated father of the jilted bride. But Natale to this day believes that the move on young Testa had but a single motive: pure envy from Little Nicky, who wanted his nephew Leonetti to command the respect given to Salvie by all.

Natale heard of a meeting in Scarfo's Atlantic City kitchen just months after the two young gangsters were made. "His venom erupted into a cascade of insults about Salvie's rise in the Philly mob, and the morals of his girlfriend. Her affairs before they met. The accusations weren't true, but Nicky spoke as if he was there. He went on and on, spewing about Salvie."

Testa, as the son of the family's longtime underboss, was raised to respect his mob superiors—even those as repugnant as Little Nicky. Despite the warning signs, he showed continued fealty to Scarfo—even carrying the boss's luggage through the Philadelphia airport when the boss returned home after a jail term for a gun charge in Texas. Young Testa was among the crew that flew back with Scarfo in January 1984.

"He was a blue blood and respected every rule of La Cosa Nostra," said Natale. "That's what killed him. He should have killed Nicky Scarfo immediately after his father's murder. But he grew up with his father as the underboss, so he knew everything about our life because he was brought up right in the middle of it. Poor Salvie put La Cosa Nostra ahead of everything. It was in Salvie's blood, and he couldn't go against the way he was raised. It's like an underground river running beneath all the homes on a block. Sooner or later, everything's gonna go."

And so it did. Scarfo's jealousy of young Testa soon exploded into murderous rage. The demented Atlantic City gangster was frustrated by his inability to reach out to the wily Testa, but he had a plan: Little Nicky reached out to Joe Pungitore, Salvie's best friend.

As Natale heard it, Scarfo bluntly explained the options to Pungitore—kill Testa or Little Nicky would "kill you, your brother, your whole family." Pungitore, terrified to stand up to Scarfo, set the wheels in motion to execute his closest friend. Salvie Testa, who had stood alongside Pungitore's father when they were initiated as made men, would now go down because of the son.

The message of impending death was delivered to Testa while he was attending a wake for Pungitore's aunt. In bizarre scene seemingly lifted from an old mob film, Scarfo's underboss Chuckie Merlino grabbed Testa's head and planted "the kiss of death" directly on the younger man's lips as he left the funeral parlor.

Pungitore recruited Salvatore "Wayne" Grande to assist in the murder plot. Grande had also sworn an oath of Mafia fealty alongside Salvie just three years earlier. And now, they were agreeing to murder their friend. Natale, decades later, remains disgusted at the way two lesser man conspired to kill one of the mob's rising stars, how far inferior mafiosi took the life of Salvie Testa.

"Instead of them—if they had balls, like men—go tell Salvie, 'This is what they want: they want to kill us, they want to kill you. What do you want to do?' Instead, they didn't say a word," Natale spits. "Wayne Grande wanted to be somebody, go up in the hierarchy of the Philadelphia family. He said, 'Don't worry, I'll bring him to the candy store. I'll kill him.' They set him up. Lowlifes. When Salvie defecated, they couldn't even be that."

On September 14, 1984, the unsuspecting Salvie Testa arrived at the candy store on Passyunk Avenue. Grande had already hidden a gun inside the cushions of a couch at the location. Pungitore had already sold out his friend. Testa was shot to death, his body wrapped in a blanket and dumped on a Jersey street, like someone putting out the trash.

The mob prince was buried in the family plot alongside his mother and father. No one was left in Nicky Scarfo's way, which was the worst thing that could have happened to his dubious regime. Left to his own devices, Scarfo was already into his gun lap as boss by late 1986, left standing among the ruins of a great family that had once held a seat on the Commission with the five New York groups.

In November, two of his top killers—Tommy DelGiorno and Nicky the Crow Caramandi—joined Team USA, becoming federal informants to testify against the head of the family. But he was still in charge when John Stanfa walked out of federal prison in the spring of 1987, unsure if the future rested in a return to the Mafia or a slab in a mortuary.

23

While John Stanfa was doing his time, each breath a reminder that he was a lucky man, his uncle John rose to become a full capo running a crew of Zips under the administration of Gambino family boss Gotti. The Queens capo ascended to the top spot by orchestrating the Christmastime killing of Castellano outside a Manhattan steak house in 1985 after Big Paul infuriated the Gotti faction with his imperious behavior. Also, Gotti's brother Gene was dealing heroin against family rules. Either way, Castellano was out and the publicity-magnet Gotti was in.

John Gambino approached the Dapper Don, hat in hand, asking if Stanfa could get a pass for his part in the Bruno execution once he left prison.

Gotti was elated by the proposal. A gift of amnesty would solidify his position atop the Gambino family, already under assault by the mighty Genovese borgata—which had put out a contract on Gotti. The quid pro quo was the full backing of the Sicilian faction going forward. Gotti saw the move as a win-win and cleared the deal to spare Stanfa. Little Nicky, outflanked but trying to save face, insisted that Stanfa never again set foot in Philadelphia—under penalty of death.

Stanfa, before even checking in with his parole officer, hustled to a Little Italy coffee shop to meet with John Gambino. The two relatives kissed each other's cheeks, with Stanfa offering his effusive thanks. Gambino explained that the clemency came with a caveat and laid out the details.

"These American gangsters are careless," Gambino said, looking his nephew directly in the eyes. "Scarfo, I hear, has no one to blame but himself. He has put himself into a tight spot. Well"—Gambino shrugged—"that's that. After all, we always heard that he never liked us Zips anyway."

Stanfa's reply was cut off by Gambino, who placed his hand close to his mouth in the old Sicilian style of delivering a message without words. Stanfa fell mute as his uncle simply continued with his thoughts.

Yes, the deal was for Stanfa to stay out of Philadelphia. So what if he instead extended an invitation for some of his old friends from the City of Brotherly Love to visit New York for a cup of espresso? Scarfo's end was near, and the future was wide-open. The first invitation went out to his fellow Bruno plotter Felix Bocchino.

Scarfo's inevitable racketeering conviction finally came down in November 1988, with the top members of his crew following him like the Pied Piper into federal penitentiaries. Little Nicky received a fifty-five-year term for thirteen murders and attempted killings during his brief and bloody reign. He was convicted in a separate trial for the 1985 murder of bookmaker "Frankie Flowers" D'Alfonso, a mob veteran aligned with the family since Bruno's early days as boss.

Scarfo's nephew Leonetti, after receiving a forty-five-year

sentence, flipped and became a federal informant. Left behind on the streets of Philadelphia were an assortment of murdered mobsters, the detritus of the savage Scarfo era.

Natale, a student of history in Philadelphia and beyond, remains stunned by the swiftness of the once-strong family's collapse: "It took over three hundred years for the many Caesars to cause the fall and decline of the great Roman Empire. It only took from the murder of Angelo Bruno in March 1980 to 1986 for Nicky Scarfo to destroy the Philadelphia La Cosa Nostra and a generation of loyal but foolish South Philadelphians who followed him, not knowing why."

The door was now wide-open for Stanfa, one of the men responsible for the undeserved death of Angelo Bruno, to march across the Walt Whitman Bridge back to South Philly. Bocchino acted as the Zip's mob "John the Baptist," spreading the word that Stanfa was coming home.

Bocchino began his missionary work after three days of scheming with Gambino and Stanfa before returning to Philly, where he visited the wife of imprisoned goodfella Joe "Chickie" Ciancaglini. Could she bring a message to Lewisburg? There was a chance, Bocchino explained, that Stanfa could become boss. If so, the three Ciancaglini sons could become made men.

No one realized this would equate to signing an order of execution for the next generation of the family in a Mafia version of Cain versus Abel, far from the Garden of Eden. Bocchino was certain that Ciancaglini the elder would jump at the chance for a new role, through the proxy of his boys, to again become part of La Cosa Nostra.

When the news reached Natale, he was both disgusted and infuriated: "The pity of it all was that no one in Philadelphia had the gumption—or for that matter, the prestige—to reach out for someone on the Commission to verify that this carpetbagger and killer would rule Philadelphia."

The toughest of the trio—and the most likely to ignore Bocchino's siren call—was Michael, who had already earned the admiration of every up-and-comer in the city. He was good with his fists, better with a knife, deadly with a gun. His best friend was "Skinny Joey" Merlino, head of his own crew and the son of Scarfo's imprisoned underboss.

Michael (Mikey Chang) was enjoying the early spring of 1989 near the recreation center on South Eighteenth and Shunk Streets when Bocchino pulled up in his Lexus. Mikey Chang, holding court outside the building, recognized Little Felix immediately. His arrival, without warning, raised hackles among the young tough guys until Ciancaglini put everyone at ease.

"It's all right," he declared. "He's a friend of my father, and one of 'those guys.'" The meaning was clear to one and all: the old man behind the wheel was a goodfella. Bocchino walked up to Michael and offered a strong handshake meant to send the message that this was a serious call. Ciancaglini, more than a half foot taller, looked down on his visitor.

Bocchino asked Mikey Chang to take a walk, placing a hand on the younger man's arm to lead him away from the assembled troops. Michael removed his arm from Bocchino's grasp before the two went on a short stroll. Bocchino explained that he was just home from New York and meeting with the Gambinos—when actually it was merely a Gambino, John.

"They have asked me to tell everybody that they are sending John Stanfa to form a new family and become the padrone, with me as his adviser on who should be included," Bocchino said before laying on the flattery. "Michael, you and your brothers plus your friend Joey Merlino were the only ones I would stand for."

Ciancaglini felt something was amiss. Wise beyond his years, he knew there was only one way to find out what it was: let Bocchino keep talking. When the twenty-minute spiel was done, Mikey Chang said he would speak with Merlino the next day, when he was planning a visit to McKean prison. He added one other thing: Ralph Natale, imprisoned there as well, would hear the same news.

"Don't take long, Michael," Bocchino advised before leaving. "They want to know in New York."

Ciancaglini later said Bocchino struck him as pure evil. Bocchino left, his job done, but painfully unaware that the young mobster had already thrown in his lot with Natale's plans to reclaim Philadelphia as his own. The next day, he would speak with Ralphy and his pal Merlino in prison to let them know about the overture.

24

A MARRIAGE OF MOB-STYLE CONVENIENCE

It was a dark, gray, and bitterly cold November day at the snow-covered Federal Correctional Institution, McKean, in Pennsylvania when a busload of forty inmates arrived after a nine-hour trip from the Ray Brook penitentiary in upstate New York near the Canadian border. The New York jail was a former Olympic Village converted into a prison.

Natale was one of the passengers taking the one-way trip. His move to the new facility came as he neared the end of his long jail term and his security level dropped. Natale remembered the thought that passed through his head after the mind-numbing trip: "Another prison. Soon I won't even know what prison I'm in." He laughed bitterly, thinking of his wife and kids—now in the same state, but still so far away.

He reflected back on his father's advice about doing time as the inmates were ordered to form two lines, where the corrections officers removed the handcuffs attached to the chains around their waists. The new arrivals, each wrapped in a federal-issued orange jumpsuit, were packed tightly into a holding pen meant to hold maybe two dozen men. The guard in charge of processing the inmates awaited, with Natale noticing his nameplate while marching past

The name rang a bell, but Natale had a lot of other things to think about. But for some unknown reason, Natale became obsessed with the guard's identity, the mystery gnawing at him. A voice in his head warned this needed to be resolved: "It's gonna be important to remember that name."

The guard called the inmates one at a time for assignment to their new residences. When Natale's name was finally announced, he approached the desk. Bingo—he remembered where he knew the name from. During his nine years in Lewisburg, a foreman at the prison had had the same last name.

After the guard and Natale exchanged greetings, Ralph said nothing more. The officer then pointed to his nameplate and asked, "Does this sound familiar to you?" He flashed a smile at the convict.

Natale noticed that the man was holding Ralph's prison records and already knew the answer. He leaned close and whispered, "We had a plumbing-shop foreman at Lewisburg with the same name, and for a hack he was quite a man."

The CO responded in the same surreptitious style: "I'm sure he will be glad to know what you think of him. He's my father."

"If you're one-tenth of what your father was to the men at Lewisburg, you'll be okay."

The second-generation hack immediately told Natale that he would land in the unit run by the young CO. The guard, after speaking by phone with his father and checking the inmate's reputation, summoned Natale the next morning. The old man had vouched for Natale as more convict than inmate, and trustworthy.

The CO now approached Natale with an offer. The CO was eager to keep his unit free of problems. Natale could help by reviewing the twice-a-month "bus list" of incoming inmates and selecting any names that fit the right criteria.

"I want guys who you know are good, not pieces of shit," he told Natale.

"You got it—I don't want them in here anyway."

Four months later, Natale spied a familiar name headed his way and heard the long-awaited if unexpected sound of opportunity knocking—loudly.

Joey Merlino was coming to McKean. "It's like hitting the lottery," he thought. "When I see his name, I thought, 'The kid's coming in.' I brought him in, I introduced him to everybody who was somebody in there."

Until that very moment, Natale's long-festering bitterness and burning desire to reclaim the mantle of the old Philadelphia mob remained a mostly abstract concept. And now, coming down on the next bus, was a Philly gangster straight from the streets, with details on mob business in their old hometown.

"I had no information at that time—who was there, who wasn't there," Natale recalled of their initially fortuitous meeting. "I thought, 'Wow, here's a godsend.' Funny, me using the word *godsend*. Maybe the devil sent him."

The processing routine was the same for Merlino as it had been for Natale, waiting while chained to the other inmates as their names were called. When the same CO summoned Joey, the guard assigned Merlino to his unit and advised, "A friend is waiting for you."

"Is it Ralphy?" asked Merlino, who was aware through the prison grapevine that Natale was at McKean.

Merlino recalled the 1982 Senate hearing, when he had

watched the marble-hard mobster uphold his sworn oath of omertà under the most difficult circumstances, at tremendous personal cost. A surge of confidence, like a jolt of electricity, filled Merlino's body.

Theirs was a May-December mob romance, star-crossed like many unions of mismatched partners. Natale's vision was clouded with dreams of redemption and revenge. Merlino's commitment to the cause was at least partially steeped in his knowledge that the bloodthirsty Scarfo, even from behind bars, wanted him dead.

After Little Nicky was jailed for life, he attempted to run the Philly family from prison through his son Nicky Jr. The family was in a shambles after Scarfo had depleted its ranks with murder after murder.

Natale, though his hatred of Scarfo burned bright, took little satisfaction from Little Nicky's demise. "To be honest, I don't want to see anyone in jail. I know Ang made me swear on my life that I wouldn't kill him—'Don't do it, Ralph!' But I wasn't happy about the conviction, not really. I wish he lives a thousand years now. He's got his own punishment. He has to get up every day and look in the mirror and see the face looking back.

"He's got a hole in his soul that can never be filled. A sick guy."

Without Scarfo on the street, the opportunity for instant mob advancement was obvious. Joey Merlino was among those who acted on his shot at the big time.

On Halloween night 1989, the younger Scarfo sat with two friends enjoying an Italian repast at Dante & Luigi's, a restaurant in South Philly. A man in a Halloween mask approached the table. Rather than a bag filled with candy, he carried a semiautomatic MAC-10 pistol. It was long rumored that the shooter was Merlino, and he pumped five bullets into Nicky Jr. The Philly mob scion collapsed as the floor became stained with his leaking blood. Incredibly, not a single bullets struck a major organ or blood vessel—and he survived.

The would-be assassin dropped his weapon on the way out, aping the infamous hit scene in *The Godfather* where Michael Corleone did the same after killing a mob boss and his NYPD crony. One informant later said that was a message to Nicky Sr., a big fan of mob movies.

Whatever the reason, Natale was unimpressed by the botched murder try: "The guy's sitting down. He had him sitting there. Joey was scared. Scared."

Nicky Sr., whose opinion mattered more than most, was convinced of Merlino's role and put a $500,000 contract on his life. Scarfo also made sure a personal message was sent to Skinny Joey that no place, behind prison bars or on the Philadelphia streets, would ever insulate him from the deranged ex-boss's deadly reach.

Publicly, Merlino put on a brave face: "Give me half a million dollars and I'll shoot myself." But Natale remembered the young thug as scared shitless.

Merlino landed in prison after a January 1990 conviction for a $350,000 armored car robbery. He faced fifteen years, but received just four from a compassionate judge worried about his mother and two sisters surviving without him. His father, noted Philly mobster Chuckie Merlino, was already doing forty-five years for his work alongside Scarfo. The elder Merlino was dispatched to die in a Texas penitentiary.

Joey Merlino was likely to do two years, then return to Philadelphia.

Natale pondered the situation as he awaited his reunion with the young wannabe gangster. Natale, accompanied by some of his close inmate pals, waited at the front entrance of Hilltop Unit 3 for Merlino. Natale donned a pair of sweatpants and a gray polo shirt for the get-together. Merlino instantly approached the older man and shook hands.

Merlino's cocky street persona was a thing of the past as he stood before Natale, who recalled Skinny Joey as frightened yet thrilled by the sight of the old gangster.

"He was scared of Scarfo," recalled Natale. "Let me put it this way—if he wasn't scared, he was crazy. He was concerned, and I could see it in his face. He looked at me like he was a drowning man and I was a branch to grab on to."

But Natale saw something else in Merlino's face, almost as if he felt guilty about something. It registered with Natale, but the moment passed.

"You don't look any different from when I last saw you in Washington," Merlino finally announced. "Boy, am I glad you're here."

Natale had his reservations about Merlino, but Ralph's single-minded focus led him to overlook any imperfections in the twenty-eight-year-old mobster: "I knew what he was, but I needed him. Listen, if I say I was hungry—I was hungry to know who was doing what on the streets. And I thought, sooner or later, I will straighten this thing out with Mr. Merlino. But let him bring these guys in."

Natale introduced Merlino all around, and he was welcomed warmly out of respect for their fellow mafioso. There was Joe Sis of the Gambinos, and Teddy from Baltimore, and even a Philly mobster named Jack Manni.

For Merlino, this was like manna from heaven. After living in a haze of fear and paranoia about the Scarfo Jr. hit, Skinny Joey had found his protector.

"They all put in for your welcome bag," said Natale. "Sweats, coffee, and of course cigarettes. The rest I put in your cell. It's next to mine. C'mon, I'll show you where we live."

Natale and his prison comrades all had single cells. And now, so did Merlino. Natale departed with a promise of extra towels and a spare pillow.

"Get that jumpsuit off and go take a shower," he told Merlino. "The water's always good and hot. When you're done, we'll have a good cup of coffee and a few doughnuts. And then, we'll talk."

Mostly, Natale planned to listen. Only then would he explain what the future held for the mob mentor, now in the position of his old pal Skinny Razor, and his unlikely new protégé. Ralph prepared for the meeting that would change everything by drinking dark coffee alone in his cell, the smell filling his nostrils with thoughts of home.

But the ambitious mobster wasn't considering his family's future together back in their old hometown. He thought instead of his long-suffering wife, Lucia, shaking his head ruefully at the memory of their sitting together in the kitchen of their old home in suburban New Jersey.

The thought passed, and he focused on the business at hand. Natale now recognized the look on his young associate's face as duplicity, bred into Merlino first by his father and then by the elder Scarfo. Natale dismissed the thought, refocusing on his long-delayed mission of redemption and reclamation.

He needed Merlino and his new breed to execute the plan of ascension to the throne of the now-scattered Philadelphia family, and to reestablish the Philly mob's seizure of

Atlantic City's riches. The first step was filling the shoes once held by old friend Angelo Bruno, and now under control of the backstabbing Stanfa.

"I knew I had to act as quickly as possible to put into action what I began to think of on the night when Angelo Bruno was killed," Natale said. He had long waited for this, never sure when or where it would occur, but always certain it would come.

That he never doubted, not for a moment.

Natale also knew Merlino ran a crew in the city, where they remained a somewhat unknown quantity even as they hung out with the top mobsters. Merlino's father, Chuckie, had been "defrocked"—booted from his position as underboss—before Scarfo went away for life on the RICO charge. Once the demotion went into effect, the younger Merlino found himself persona non grata in the close-knit world of the local Cosa Nostra.

Natale felt one other thing in his bones, one that should have caused him to pause before plunging ahead: Merlino was cut from the same untrustworthy cloth as Testa and Scarfo, the dead and the jailed successors to Bruno. Instead Natale threw caution to the winds, focused on taking back what was rightfully his.

Merlino finally knocked on the cell door. Each man took a seat before the host stood to prepare a fresh pot of coffee and bring out the doughnuts. "Now you can bring me up-to-date about what's going on in our hometown," Natale said.

The ball was now in Merlino's court; he could spill his guts or play things close to the vest. Natale had a feeling that things would play out the way he wanted, and Skinny Joey would sign on with Team Ralph. But the younger man had been schooled by his father about the ways of the Philadelphia

From a young age, Ralph Natale saw the future: "Even as a kid I wanted to be a boss, and I did just that."

Put 'em up: Ralph at age nine, already in training for life's hard knocks.

A teenage Ralph with twenty-year-old Lucy, just one year into a marriage now in its seventh decade.

A young Ralph behind the stick at The Friendly Tavern, owned by his friend and mob mentor John "Skinny Razor" DiTullio.

Boys' night out: Ralph (standing center, with a mustache) with an assortment of friends from organized labor and organized crime.

Ralph with (from left) Frank Vadino and Felix Bocchino, letting the good times roll in a South Jersey bar. Bocchino was later one of the plotters behind the murder of Ralph's friend and Philly mob boss Angelo Bruno.

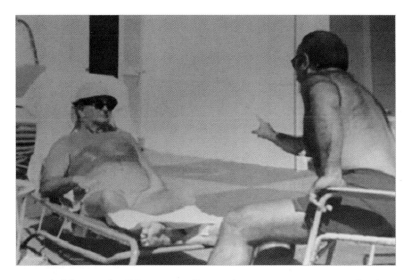

In Ralph's words: "[Raymond] Turchi was a great union leader [the president of Union 301] and as he got older he wanted to be something that he wasn't. He got very carried away with his ideas during a convention at my Palm Springs home and I had to have a talk with him. I said, 'Ray, sit down or you'll never get a chance to get back up.'"

(Right to left) Ralph's close friend and associate Edward T. Hanley, general president of the International Hotel and Restaurant Workers Union, with union secretary-treasurer John Gibson and Ralph at the Palm Springs housewarming party. Ralph's luxurious home was on the Palm Springs Country Club golf course, inside a gated community.

Legendary Teamsters boss Jimmy Hoffa (second from left) with his guests at a Washington, D.C., banquet for the union big-wig. Also pictured, Ralph's driver and trusted associate Frank Vadino (far left).

(Right to left) Ralph with Buffalo mobster John Sacco, Philly hitman Frank Gambino, and Ronald Turchi at the Lewisburg Penitentiary. Ralph later testified against Gambino.

Ralph and Joseph "Pepe" Marino, a Staten Island holdup man convicted in a 1978 armored-car heist that netted $2.25 million.

Ralph with Philly mobster Jimmy DePasquale (second from left) and (far right) top methamphetamine maker Adrian Mastrangello Jr.

Ralph with Jimmy Flynn, a reputed member of Whitey Bulger's infamous Winter Hill Gang in Boston. Flynn later changed careers, and played a judge in the Oscar-winning movie *Good Will Hunting*.

Genovese crime family member Vito Alberti (left) and Ralph's future Philly consigliere Ronald Turchi (right) inside United States Penitentiary, Lewisburg.

Ralph with fellow inmate Sam Mason (center), who became like a brother to the mob boss, and Ronald Turchi (right). All three were members of the Lewisburg penitentiary fire department.

Jack Jennings, known to his fellow inmates as "Cuban Jack," was once a trainer for Cuban leader Fidel Castro's elite inner circle of bodyguards. He is pictured leaning against the pole with his hand on Ralph's left shoulder. Jennings has his other arm around Ronald Turchi, and the man on the other side of the pole is feared Buffalo enforcer John Sacco.

Thomas Andretta (bottom right) is one of the men long suspected in the abduction and murder of Jimmy Hoffa.

Philip "Rusty" Rastelli, boss of New York's Bonanno family. Ralph asked Rastelli to take a photo once he left prison, and Phil sent this photo to Ralph's wife.

Cosa Nostra, to never reveal his true feeling about any mob business to anyone.

The pair eventually sat side by side, like a penitent confessing to the parish priest. The older man spoke first. "Tell me, Joey, who appears to be in charge of anything—including Atlantic City—since they put Little Nicky away?" Natale sensed immediately that Merlino grasped the unspoken message that Ralph intended to retake the city as his own. And maybe, just maybe, their own.

An obviously pleased Merlino replied without haste, merging his future with Natale's vision for a mob rebirth in the City of Brotherly Love. "Ralphy, nobody has attempted to put anything together except maybe Nicky Jr., as far as I know. Michael [Ciancaglini] and I have a few sports books turning in to us, and a couple of numbers books from the yams"—a reference to the Black Mafia. "But that's it."

This raised the first red flag for Natale. Merlino was a well-known "beat artist," hiding behind his father's fearsome rep to stiff bookies on his deep gambling debts. None of the city's gambling operators would trust the degenerate gambler with their money.

"You can't buy a reputation," Natale said bluntly in recalling their conversation. "You have to earn it. And in Merlino's case, that was impossible. Nobody of worth trusted him, on the street or in prison. And that included his family and friends."

So Merlino, his credibility shot, needed Ralphy far more than the mob veteran needed him. Natale owned credibility in spades, even after all his time off the streets, with his ties to the men who had first formed the family—Bruno and Skinny Razor—and his contacts inside the five families of New York.

Everything was falling into place. Natale was certain that he could forge Merlino and his crew into a hammer to swing hard in his best interests. But he had one final question about Joey's pal Ciancaglini:

"Is Michael capable?" Translation: Is Michael a killer?

"Ralph, he banged out his first when he was sixteen," Merlino replied breathlessly. "He's got a fearsome reputation throughout South Philly, with or without a gun. Ralphy, you'll love him. He's like your old partner used to be."

Natale enjoyed the reference to his old hatchet-wielding compatriot Mike Marrone. High praise, he thought to himself. "If your Michael is half the man that Mike Marrone was," he finally said, "he'll do."

Ciancaglini, like Merlino, was already surrounded by a street crew. The good news kept getting better. Natale, like a surrogate father, finally reached over and placed his open palm on top of Merlino's hand. There was one final question.

"Is Michael on your visiting list?"

The answer was yes. Natale told his young charge to bring Ciancaglini up to McKean for a sit-down as soon as possible.

"I'll have my daughter and wife visit on the same day so we can talk on the visit," Natale said. "Now, finish your doughnuts, and I'll show you where everything is at—including 'our' TV room and the chairs only for 'us.'"

Merlino departed with a considerably rosier view of his future and the world outside the prison walls. For Natale, the key was Ciancaglini, a son in a notorious mob clan. His dad, Joseph "Chickie" Ciancaglini, was of Ralph's generation, a onetime Teamster enforcer and a straight-up killer. He took a bullet during one labor dispute and lived to tell the tale.

His rise through the Philadelphia family was aided in large measure by his decision to sell out Sindone in the Bruno assassination, and he wound up behind bars for more than three decades after serving under Scarfo. Among Chickie's crimes was the ice-pick murder of a rival gangster.

"We grew up together," Natale said of the family patriarch. "Went to Bartlett Junior High. At that time, when I was rising, he knew everybody. He was a goon for Local 107. They were fighting at the time, and somebody shot him with a small caliber—you can catch them, almost. Hit him, but didn't do nothing."

His boys followed him into the family business—Mikey and Joey Ciancaglini, who wound up on opposite sides of the mob war soon instigated by Natale and Skinny Joey.

"Mikey Chang was a gangster," Natale recalled with admiration. "He was the closest thing to Salvie Testa. Mikey was maybe six foot one, up and down. The kid could fight with his hands, and he could shoot, too. But a nice kid, a handsome kid. Not a bully, but tough as they come. Made for me."

Natale continued preaching the Gospel of Ralph to new recruit Merlino, who hung on every word, every promise. Philadelphia would soon be theirs, and Atlantic City, too. Ralph would serve as the boss, and Joey as his right-hand man and underboss.

"We did a lot of talking," explained Natale. "We swore to one another, hugged and kissed one another. I told him, 'This is gonna get serious, Joey. When I come home, there's gonna be a lot of action.' He nodded, but shaky. And I said, 'If nothing's done, when I get home, I'm gonna clean it up myself.' He said, 'I know, my father told me about you.'"

The pair also entered into a pact that the once-betrayed

Natale considered a sacrosanct vow: no matter how it turned out, if somebody wound up back behind bars or in the ground, the man left on the outside would make sure the other's family was not forgotten. Natale didn't want a repeat of his first jail term, with promises broken and his wife left to fend for herself.

"With Merlino, that meant I'd take care of his girl, his mother, and his two sisters," Natale recalled nearly twenty-five years later. "That meant to me that you make sure, no matter what. 'Cause we were gonna do a little work. There's gonna be a lot of problems. I said, 'You remember, 'cause somebody might get lucky with a shot at me. I don't intend it to happen, but you know . . .'"

Mikey Chang, accompanied by his girlfriend and another tough kid named Tommy "Horsehead" Scafidi, made the trip to McKean two weeks after the initial Merlino-Natale summit. Ralph's wife came with two of his daughters to the decent-size visitors' room, where inmates were permitted to sit with the guests of other inmates. The guards, focused on the arrival of Ciancaglini's attractive companion Caryn, paid little attention to the other guests.

Scafidi—his nickname came from his equine profile, not the infamous scene from *The Godfather*—boasted a mob lineage like Ciancaglini. Scafidi's brother Tori was a made man, and his grandfather was involved in the Mafia. Despite the odd alias, he was good-looking with typically slicked-back black hair. He stayed with Caryn as Natale sat down with his fellow inmate and Ciancaglini.

Natale looked intently at Michael's face as the two men shook hands, looking for any sign of duplicity. Instead, he saw honesty and courage. "This one's a keeper," Natale thought to himself as he laid out the plot first conjured in a

Florida prison on the night of the Bruno assassination. He specifically mentioned taking back Local 54, a potential gold mine awaiting them in Atlantic City.

Once they had control of the roughly twenty-two thousand union members, Natale explained, the family would run the health insurance and severance pension funds. The mob would take $100 per month per member in kickbacks from the insurance brokers running the twin funds. The smiles grew on the young duo's faces as they did the crooked math.

Three mob bosses had died for the pot of gold at the end of Atlantic City's rainbow. And now it was about to land in their laps. This was the time for Natale to find out exactly how serious Mikey Chang and Skinny Joey were about doing what now needed to be done.

The three men walked to an outside visiting area, where Natale lit up one of his favorite H. Upmann cigars, brought as a gift by Ciancaglini. A chill was in the spring air as they stood together. The younger men had heard tales of Natale from their relatives, but they would hear firsthand this day exactly what the old hand was capable of doing.

Natale bit off the end of his cigar before carefully lighting up, rolling the smoke to get the perfect ash—a trick learned in his youth. As he spoke, the other two leaned in so as not to miss a word.

"First things first. Michael, do you have the type of men who are ready to do what has to be done? Remember, the greater the fortune, the greater the risk. There are many people from the New York families who—if they become aware of what's really at stake—will be willing to risk their lives or take lives if necessary for that amount of money.

"We must act now, before anyone else becomes aware of

what can be done in Atlantic City. With your help, this will be ours again."

Natale assured the two that Chicago would back their play in return for his years of silence while behind bars. And he explained, looking at Michael and ignoring Joey, that the process would require bloodshed and a big set of balls. It would also start immediately.

"We must take back the streets of South Philly with a bang and send that message to everyone who is sniffing what belongs to us," Natale said. "Remember, Michael, I'm doing this sentence for some people in New York as well as Philadelphia. It's important that I show real strength from here in prison, so when the time comes, the Commission will recognize us."

Michael had a question: "Ralph, do you want us to let everybody know, no matter who they are, what we intend to do?"

"Without a doubt," Ralph shot back. "Because that's the only way to find out who the snakes are, and as sure as the day follows night, they will show themselves. And then, my young friend, if you're the man Joey says you are, you won't have to take a ride back here for me to tell you what must be done. After you do what you have to do, all the snakes will disappear."

Ralph was almost done with his young acolytes, who sat mesmerized as he spoke. Natale asked a final question about the street situation in the city: Was anybody running his mouth about taking control of the family with Scarfo behind bars?

Ciancaglini immediately mentioned "Louie Irish" De-Luca, operator of an after-hours club and a downtown drug dealer. DeLuca was palling around with Natale's old sidekick

Ronnie Turchi and was bad-mouthing both Merlino and Ciancaglini—"chirping inside his club whenever he gets high, in front of anybody who will listen," Michael reported.

Natale smiled and began to speak softly, almost as if reciting poetry. But his words sounded more like an obituary: "Louie Irish, with his own words like many egotistical men, composed his own epitaph. So, Michael, when you finally take all of his thoughts and dreams from him, everybody who mistakenly thought he was somebody will know it came from the people he talked about. And those people made him a nobody."

The meeting was finished, and the two young mobsters were on board. Natale stood between Merlino and Ciancaglini, his hands on their arms, as they marched in unison toward the visiting room. Ciancaglini took Ralph's advice to heart: strike fast, and strike hard.

At 1:00 a.m. on May 24, 1990, as DeLuca drove his burgundy 1986 Cadillac toward home, the Natale faction lashed out. Two shooters surprised Louie Irish, blasting through his car windshield at the helpless businessman. Three of the gunshots found their mark, and the fifty-four-year-old club owner was dead. He was unarmed, with $129 cash in his pockets. Mikey Chang, living up to his advance billing, was one of the gunmen.

Those were the first bullets fired in Natale's quest to take everything back. They were far from the last. The killing of Louie Irish sent a message, but many others had a higher rank on Natale's hit list of revenge. The top spot for a bullet unquestionably belonged to John Stanfa, one of the conspirators in the 1980 killing of Bruno. For Natale, getting rid of the man who killed his beloved and respected boss was nearly as exciting as the prospect of becoming the boss.

"That stuck in my craw," Natale said of Stanfa's role in the murder. "I thought for years, 'When I get home, I'm gonna kill him and everybody around him.' The young guys knew—their fathers and their uncles told them, 'Ralphy's crazy. He talks nice, but he's crazy. He'll kill him right then and there.' And I would have, 'cause he was involved in it. I sent word back to the street, 'I'm gonna kill them.' That was on record. And history rolls on."

Another prime target was off the streets: Scarfo, who'd run the family into the ground while lining his pockets and stiffing Lucia.

"I really wanted to kill Scarfo," Natale continued. "I know that sounds terrible, but that's how I felt. And it would have gotten done. I wasn't Superman, but I was pretty good at my job. Or he woulda killed me. I know that. But I never thought it could happen."

Natale arranged the murder of two other mobsters to ease his eventual return to the streets. Felix Bocchino, the man who delivered the shotgun that killed Angelo Bruno, was gunned down on January 29, 1992, by Mikey Chang after trying to shake down Merlino's uncle "Sheiky" Baldino. Ciancaglini visited Natale in prison to deliver the news of his ultimate rebuke to Bocchino's overtures on behalf of Stanfa.

Bocchino was shot four times in the head through his car window. It was a textbook hit: fast, economical, lethal.

Four months later to the day, James "Jimmy Brooms" DiAddorio was shot to death while speaking on the phone at the end of the bar inside the Vulpine Athletic Club in Philadelphia. Two men wearing black hats pumped a half dozen bullets into the helpless victim, who made the mistake of openly pledging his allegiance to the Stanfa faction—often loudly, after a few drinks in local bars.

The murder was done strictly as a message that the Natale faction was coming and anyone standing in their way faced the same fate.

One more vitally important detail had to be handled: Natale didn't want to make a move without some sort of approval from the Commission in New York. The proposition was dicey at best, given that he had a few years left on his arson and drug convictions.

But fortune and the federal prison system smiled on Natale. He was transferred to Danbury, Connecticut, where his fellow inmates included onetime Lucchese family boss Vic Amuso and Raymond Patriarca Jr., son of the legendary New England crime boss.

Amuso reached out to Natale, and the two sat together in Amuso's cell drinking coffee and eating Entenmann's doughnuts—"That was a big deal," Natale remembered.

The next night, the mobsters from New York, Philadelphia, and New England gathered for a chat. Natale, cards close to his prison jumpsuit, launched into his Stanfa gambit. Natale asked Amuso to send a message to jailed Gambino boss Gotti asking whether Stanfa's regime was sanctioned by New York.

Amuso, convicted in the infamous New York "Windows" prosecution, interrupted Natale: "He can't be the boss. We had a meeting, all the new bosses, when they sent the old Commission away. The first rule they made was no foreign-born Italian mafiosi of La Cosa Nostra could ever be a boss in the United States. So I know he's not the boss."

Natale asked if there was a way to find out how Stanfa

was approved. It turned out approval came from John Gambino, his relative and the Italian-born Gambino capo. When an intermediary finally posed the question to Gotti, the Dapper Don dismissed the Philly pretender.

"John Stanfa?" Gotti sniffed. "Who knows him?"

That was good enough for Natale, who told his young underlings that the word had come down from on high—Stanfa could not serve as boss. Natale's new cohorts—including Merlino, sprung from prison in April 1992—seemed unable to grasp the enormity of this decree directly from two members of the mob's highest authority.

"When I told those idiots, when I sent word, they said, 'It can't be!'" Natale recalled with a tone of incredulity. "They didn't believe me. Mikey Chang was allowed to visit me, and I said, 'Listen—this is what Vic Amuso told me: He is not the boss. He never will be. He will not be the boss in a million years.' Stanfa had no right to make anybody. He was never the boss."

Natale then gave Ciancaglini specific and savage instructions on dealing with Stanfa in his absence. "I told Michael, when this punk John Stanfa calls to meet you, you make sure you and Joey go in there loaded up." I knew Stanfa would call them because that's what the Sicilians do! And I said as soon as they open the doors to let you in, kill everybody. The city's ours. They didn't do that because Joey Merlino talked Michael out of it. Merlino was broke when he got home, so he told Michael, 'Come on, we'll go and shake guys down and use Stanfa's name. And when Ralph comes home, I'll tell him.'

"Michael says, 'But Ralph told me . . .' And Joey said, 'Don't worry about it. He ain't coming home for a while.'"

So, when Merlino sat down with Stanfa on April 28,

1992, the pretender to the mob throne walked away unscathed. "And don't Michael get killed by Stanfa?" Natale said.

He did, in a manner worthy of Shakespearean tragedy. The Stanfa-Natale war left the Ciancaglini family a house bitterly divided as Michael threw in with Ralphy while his brother Joey remained aligned with the ruling regime as its underboss. According to Natale, big brother Joey fired the first shot in the family feud in March 1992.

"Mikey claimed his brother had set him up," Natale recounted. "Two North Jersey guys were in a car with his brother. He came home from the gym to his house, and he heard a car door slam, and he saw the two guys. They shot the windows out of the house, where Mikey's wife and young kids lived. He claimed his brother was in the car. So you gotta do what you gotta do."

Mikey Chang escaped by diving through the front door as the shotgun blasts tore up the brick façade of his home.

The reciprocal deed was done on March 2, 1993, as Joey Ciancaglini arrived to open his Warfield Breakfast & Lunch Express shortly before 6:00 a.m. An FBI surveillance camera captured the grisly sights and sounds—thirty seconds of gunfire and the screams of a waitress after several men were seen bursting in on their stunned target.

Joey Ciancaglini, shot five times in the ear, cheek, and eye, incredibly survived the hit attempt. He fought with the medics trying to save his life and was handcuffed before the EMTs could load him onto a stretcher and into the ambulance. The killers, to Natale's continued incredulity, fled the scene with their target still breathing.

"They didn't know how to kill him," former hit man Natale said bluntly. "They shot him, but he lived. These things happen. And Michael didn't shoot his brother—that's bullshit. He wasn't there."

Ciancaglini was left permanently crippled—blind in one eye, deaf in one ear, both physically and mentally disabled, left to walk with a cane. His Stanfa colleagues were left to handle the payback, with the Sicilian-born boss caught on a wiretap in the spring that year ordering the murders of Mikey Chang, Merlino, Natale, and fellow mafioso Gaeton Lucibello.

Stanfa had specific directions: Merlino and Ciancaglini were to be buried in quick-drying cement, and Lucibello's tongue was to be cut out. He called for a "welcome home" treat for Natale once the old-school mobster walked out of prison.

"He's gotta go," Stanfa announced. "I don't even want to give him time to breathe the air."

Ciancaglini never saw his concrete coffin—or the bullet that killed him. On August 5, 1993, as Mikey Chang and Joey Merlino walked along Catharine Street around 1:30 p.m., two shooters in baseball caps opened fire in a brazen daylight mob hit. Ciancaglini died from a single bullet that struck him in the arm—and wound up hitting his heart.

Merlino was shot in the legs and buttocks, a clear indication of the shooters' ineptitude. The killers sped off in a waiting car that was dumped and torched about thirty-five blocks away. The missed opportunity to whack Skinny Joey was emblematic of Stanfa's dopey crew: Another proposed hit by the family failed when the hit man loaded his shotgun with the wrong-size shells. And a previous murder plot against Merlino featured a onetime exotic dancer brought aboard to slip cyanide into his drink at a nightclub. That one failed as well.

Natale believes Merlino bears the blame for Ciancaglini's murder: "Joey made the snowballs, and he had Michael throw them. Poor Michael got killed because he didn't listen to me."

Natale was in the prison weight room working out when he heard about Ciancaglini's violent demise. The distraught don dropped a forty-pound weight on his finger, taking the tip right off.

"All I felt was the pain of missing him," Natale recalled. "I felt sick to my stomach and I thought, 'I'm gonna straighten this out.'"

But Natale didn't feel any guilt about enlisting young Mikey Chang to the cause of his redemption: "I didn't feel responsible for his death. This was my life, and that was his life. I did what I did, and I was responsible for my life. We're all responsible for our own lives."

Vengeance came quickly—if not successfully. On the morning of August 31, Stanfa was riding with his son Joe in a Cadillac Seville when a van with gun holes carved into its side pulled alongside on the Schuylkill Expressway and opened fire. The twenty-three-year-old Joe was hit in the face, with a bullet lodging behind his cheekbone. One of the Cadillac's tires was blown out, with driver Fred Aldrich somehow steering the crippled car to safety. Aldrich predictably told the cops that he saw nothing.

Natale was stunned that his young charges had somehow missed their target. "I wanted to kill John Stanfa, not his son. The guy who was supposed to shoot Stanfa missed and hit the son. Dopey bastards. The kid got shot accidentally. All you have to do is block the car from the front, get another car right behind, and somebody gets out and shoots. End of story."

The botched Stanfa hit turned the Philly war into national news, with *The New York Times* weighing in with a piece on the battle for the family leadership. "Philadelphia Braces for Increase in Mob Violence," read their typically understated headline. It took barely two weeks for the Natale faction to lash out again, with Stanfa loyalist Leon "Yonnie" Lanzilotti shot in the face as he walked along Eighth Street in South Philly. Police said the diminutive bookmaker was ambushed by three ski-masked shooters who left him to die.

Thought his blood flowed like a red river along the sidewalk, Lanzilotti survived the murder try. The new generation of gangsters had twice lived up to their mocking reputation as "the gang that couldn't shoot straight," to quote the classic Jimmy Breslin mob book.

Before finally coming home, Natale had a strange encounter in Danbury. One of his fellow inmates was Benjamin "Lefty Guns" Ruggiero, the unfortunate mafioso who brought FBI undercover Joe Pistone into the Bonanno family to disastrous results (and a hit movie where Ruggiero was played by Al Pacino). When the two men met, Natale felt that the past was the past. They were still a couple of made men in the same prison. Respect was due, and given.

"I never mentioned the streets," Natale recounted. "We shook hands, we hugged. The hug was a problem with some of the made guys, who still remembered how he brought a rat in. I stood up for him and told all those guys—I mean, I was me in those days—you oughta be ashamed of yourself."

In 1993, as Natale prepared from his release from prison and ascension to boss, news reached Ralph about the turncoat Charlie Allen. Karma had come finally knocking for the treacherous onetime member of the Natale crew.

The informer went into the Witness Protection Program, living in a leafy Virginia suburb under the name William

Terry. He was married to a woman with a stepdaughter—and she came forward that year with allegations that Allen had sexually abused her for thirteen years, starting when she was a four-year-old.

Allen told the girl that if she ever said one word, he would execute her mother and grandmother—and force her to watch the killings.

Charlie Allen was convicted of rape and sodomy. A judge sentenced him to forty-five years in prison, where he died of cancer.

"He had a nice little home, he was living with a woman," said Natale. "This is where he shoulda ended. But this is where he ended: Full of cancer, in the joint. That's what he was."

25

DON'T CALL IT A COMEBACK

Natale returned home on September 23, 1994, breathing the fresh air of a free man for the first time in sixteen years. Once his lungs were filled, his eyes grew wide with anticipation: The paroled Natale was determined to restore the family and retrieve what was taken from him. For some, the reality is never as sweet as the dream that preceded it. That was not the case for Ralph Natale. He assumed the mantle of family leadership as if slipping into a pair of old slippers, sliding comfortably into the seat without a second thought, his destiny fulfilled.

"I felt like I was born for it," he said. "That simple. Because I did what I had to do, I got all the requirements, and here I am. And I didn't give nobody up. That's part of the record. There was no way I would come back and walk away from things. Why would I? I just did sixteen straight years, lost everything that I had. Atlantic City was thriving."

He even reached out to his old union pal Ed Hanley with word that he intended to seize control of the local unions once more.

"Guess what he said? 'With my blessing.' Why wouldn't he?" said Natale. "He didn't have to do a day. They wanted him in the worst way in that Senate hearing."

There was a bon voyage celebration at the prison, hosted by Genovese capo Federico "Fritzy" Giovanelli—accused of killing a New York detective. "What a send-off," Natale remembered. "Fritzy and all the made guys. You never saw anything like it. Sandwiches, sodas. What a scene."

A homecoming party was thrown by his family, with various generations of the Natale clan in attendance. Natale was barred from Philadelphia, so the fête was hosted elsewhere by his aunt Dolly—mother of the turncoat Raymond Bernard.

"She saw me, she said, 'Ralphy, can I talk to you?'" he recalled. "We hugged and we kissed. And she said to me, 'Ralphy, don't kill Raymond.' 'Cause she knew what he did, cost me all those years. I said, 'Kill him?' How could I kill my aunt Dolly's son? I can't do that. Figure that one out. I can't do that."

Absent from the party was nemesis Stanfa, already behind bars on a racketeering rap. He was arrested and jailed in March 1994, convicted the next year, and sentenced to die behind bars. Natale would never get a shot at his number one nemesis.

Philly's Black Mafia also arrived at Ralphy's Pennsauken, New Jersey, penthouse, bearing a multicolored robe as a welcome-home gift. Their cohorts doing time in Lewisburg had vouched for the new Philly boss as a stand-up guy.

"I don't know how much they paid for it," he still marvels. "And they told me, 'If you need us, we are here for you.' They asked for permission to visit with some friends of mine, and I said, 'Come right up.' They loved that, and why not?

They knew my reputation, and I knew theirs. They were all gentlemen, straight up. My wife was there!"

The new boss remembers their assurance that he would have their support in all endeavors. "They said, 'We got your back, let us know,'" he recalled. "And I said, 'Hey, I ain't that old, you know?'"

One and all shared a good laugh before the guests headed out. But Natale was now the head of the most dysfunctional crime family in the United States, and perhaps in the long history of American organized crime—not that it felt that way to him.

"There's only one boss in Philadelphia," he declared after leaving prison. "That's Ralph Natale, and that's where the fuck it's at."

Natale once again set up shop at the racetrack in Cherry Hill, operating with impunity out of the Currier & Ives restaurant. He was astounded and delighted after all his time away by the discovery of simulcasting: "Even when the track was closed, you could bet on all the races from every track. That was something new to me—wow, you can bet everything!"

He was at the track as usual one afternoon when an old friend appeared to offer his assistance to the new boss.

"Blinky Palermo came up to see me, with his driver Red—I never knew his real name!" Natale recalled with delight about the reunion. "Blinky looked pretty good, but he's old—ninety-one, ninety-two years old. They come up wearing the old double-breasted suits—clean, with the white shirts, immaculate. We hugged, we kissed, we had lunch. We laughed.

"And then he leaned over to me—he was a shooter, he buried a few people, you know? Out in the street, whatever. And he said, 'You know, I'm still capable.'

"Oh, I loved him. He meant it! I said, 'I know. Don't you dare think I don't. Let these young punks do what they gotta do. We'll see what they got.' And in the end, they didn't have too much in them, as men."

Palermo was an anomaly among the men who made up the Philadelphia mob of the 1990s. The high-rolling Natale was stunned by the way his new associates carried themselves—living at home with their mothers, driving other people's cars, working nickel-and-dime scams.

"They were all dead out," Natale recounted. "But what am I gonna do—use mannequins? I needed somebody."

One of his first decisions in the top seat came back to bite him. A soldier named Ronnie Previte—a rotund ex–Philadelphia police officer—was with the Stanfa faction, and Merlino agitated for his murder. Natale was unconvinced by his young partner's arguments.

"When I came home, I hooked up with Ronnie," Natale recalled. "We used to hang out. Joey Merlino wanted to kill everybody—including Previte. I said, 'Did this guy ever do anything with a gun? . . . No? Then it's over. That's enough killing. You can't kill everybody.' Previte wasn't a shooter. Well, I let him live. And he came up wired at the racetrack, recorded everything."

A busy Natale set quickly to reestablishing the family's preeminent role in the Philadelphia underworld, ignoring the conditions of his parole—strict guidelines about where he could go and whom he could see. He reached out to the owner of a banquet hall on Front Street, typically used for weddings and other family parties. Natale had a different kind of party in mind.

"First we had a big meeting in the family," he recalled. "I said, 'Who took all the action? The numbers, the bookmaking, the loan-sharking?' And they told me: 'This guy has this, this guy has that.' I said, 'Hold on one second.'"

He arranged for a weekday event at the hall, catered with plenty of food and booze. Then he dispatched his mob minions to contact every bookie, loan shark, and numbers hustler in the city and issue an invitation that none dared decline—directly from Natale. "I said, 'Tell them I'm asking.' See, they didn't trust Joey Merlino. When he used to bet, he'd lose the whole bank. Everybody knew him—he was like John Gotti, he didn't pay. Now I'm saying, 'Tell 'em Ralphy wants to see 'em. Tell them I want to see them all, and if I have to call again, there's gonna be a problem.' Because they knew my reputation before I went to Lewisburg. They knew what I meant, and they all show up."

The buffet and an open bar awaited, as did Natale, with his underboss Merlino and consigliere Turchi. The new ruling triumvirate put their guests at ease before bringing them into a room, one at a time, where the mood was far less welcoming.

Natale did the talking. He wasted no words in laying out the new rules. None of the visitors saw the weapon he carried in case additional persuasion was needed.

"I'm gonna talk," he said by way of opening. "It's not for you to talk. When I ask you a question, you have to answer. I know what you're doing. I'm not here to put you out of business."

Natale would summon one of his underlings to join the party—and resume the monologue. "You know him? He's your new partner. Now, if you need money, ask him. We'll make sure you get that money—for a certain fee. But he's your partner for all your action, and nobody can fuck with you for the rest of your life."

Natale, once finished, flashed a Cheshire cat grin. Each and every attendee responded the same way to his proposal. "Every one of them said it sounds fair. And I said, 'It is fair!' Because I always began and ended with this: 'Everything illegal in the city of Philadelphia belongs to La Cosa Nostra. That's us. Our friends die, our relatives die, because of this. Get that through your head. Never think different. If not, you have a problem.'

"They knew I woulda killed them. If I had to, I woulda banged one of them right in the head, just to make sure."

His ragtag mob army was soon reaping the financial benefits: BMWs, big-screen TVs. Life was good until it wasn't.

Natale's inclusion of Turchi in his mob administration provided a perfect illustration of his mob acumen: His old pal had plotted to kill Ralphy once he came back to the city. Word of the planned hit reached Natale two days after he came home, when the kid hired by Turchi as the shooter was overheard discussing the murder plot in a Philadelphia pizzeria.

The wise old head remembered the adage to keep your friends close and your enemies closer. There was a personal aspect, too: he had known Turchi since the days when the young mobster played shortstop at Southern High, getting drafted by the Phillies. His career ended two weeks later when Turchi stabbed a man in a bar fight. And the two were convicted together in the Mr. Living Room arson. Turchi took the hit and did his time and never opened his mouth.

"I made him the consigliere because I felt sorry for him," Natale said. "He thought he was more than everybody. He was a killer—stone-cold. But how can I kill him? I knew him since I was a kid. He might want to kill me, but he'd never be a rat. Turchi? Never."

Ralphy was right: Turchi went to his grisly death in October 1999 without ever speaking to the feds. His naked body was found facedown in the trunk of a car, his hands and feet bound, with two bullets to his head—which was wrapped in a plastic bag to prevent any blood spatter.

"They told him they were gonna make him, and they killed him," recalled Natale—a scene right out of *Goodfellas,* where Joe Pesci's character was dispatched in similar fashion.

Natale, decades after his initiation ceremony with Gambino and Bruno, agreed to be remade when Merlino approached him with an invite to become a made man. Though unnecessary, Natale accepted the offer in the interest of keeping the peace among his factions. The ceremony was held in a suite at the Hilton Hotel near Veterans Stadium, with a gun and a knife in the room.

Both men swore an oath of omertà to the family. And each acknowledged their souls "would burn in hell" if they broke their word.

"I never told him, that punk, that I was already made by the two biggest guys," Natale said. "But he wanted to show everybody what he had—Ralph Natale. None of them would have gone near Joey Merlino if he didn't have Ralphy."

Given the option, Natale said, "I wouldn't have made him." The boss nevertheless embraced Merlino as second-in-command of the family, even making a public proclamation that Skinny Joey was under his personal umbrella of protection.

"What was I gonna do by myself?" he offered in self-defense. "Go out on the streets and take numbers personally? I told everybody, 'If you think you're gonna get near that kid, you're gonna have to kill me first.' And then he forgot that I put my life on the line for him."

Once Natale was embraced as the new boss, a summons came from the Gambino family for a sit-down. The New Yorkers had backed Stanfa from the start, and they were now waving a white flag.

"Me, Joey, and Ronnie Turchi took a ride up to New York," said Natale. "Gotti was in jail, and they had three top captains running the family. They asked me to do them a favor: please don't kill Mikey Chang's brother or Stanfa's son. I said, 'Why kill them? Okay.' Then they brought me in the back—'Ralphy, you gave your word. . . .' I said, 'Don't say any more. My word is good.'"

Natale wasn't surprised by the call for compassion for the two survivors of the war: "Lots of times it happens that if a guy survives a hit, they'll give you a pass."

The first target once Natale landed in Philadelphia was William Veasey, killed just before his brother—mob capo John Veasey—was scheduled to testify in a mob trial about the murder of Ciancaglini and a failed hit on Merlino. The man known as Billy was gunned down on October 5, 1995, after picking up doughnuts on his way to work.

Ralph later testified that one of the killers was a third Ciancaglini brother, John. The killing of William Veasey was direct payback for the Mikey Chang murder—"It was brother for a brother," Natale told the FBI.

The next bump in the road for the Natale regime came from Northern New Jersey, where capo Joseph Sodano operated as a major earner for the Philly group: illegal video poker machines, loan-sharking, and fencing stolen goods. Natale heard from his friends in New York that Sodano was also working with some of the families in the city, rather than exclusively for him. This did not sit well with Natale.

The new boss summoned all the Philadelphia-connected guys in Newark to come south and sit face-to-face. Sodano, to his detriment, declined the invitation—instead sending a cash-stuffed envelope back to Natale with mobster Philip "Philly Fay" Casale.

"Full of Franklins," Natale recalled. "I said, 'Bring it back to him. Tell him I want to see him man to man.' Philly said, 'Ralph, this guy thinks you want to kill him.' I said that his underwear must be dirty. That's the old saying: 'You never show up if your underwear's dirty.' I said, 'Tell him nobody wants to kill him.'"

"And he never came."

Now somebody wanted to kill him. Natale instructed family associate Peter "Pete the Crumb" Caprio that the clock was running: Sodano must be killed within a week.

"I sent word: 'Pete, if he's not dead within a week, I'm gonna come out of retirement and I'm gonna show you how to do it. I'm gonna embarrass all of you—and who knows what else I'm gonna do while I'm up there,'" Natale recalled. "He knew what I meant. Sodano was dead within a week."

Sodano, with two bullets to the head, was found behind the wheel of his SUV, left in the parking lot of a Newark senior citizens complex on December 7, 1996. The contract went to Casale, who wasted little time in tracking his target down.

When the Crumb flipped and joined the feds, he recalled Natale's exact order: "We got to bang this guy out."

Only a few months earlier, Natale endured one of his darker days with the death of an old mob friend. He was at the track in May 1996 when Palermo's driver appeared late one afternoon. The boss was holding court in the clubhouse— "nice room, hundred-dollar window, fifty-dollar window, free food," he recalled. "At about four thirty, I'm buying everyone drinks. And as soon as I saw Red, I knew Blinky died. I had that feeling.

"He comes over: 'I've got bad news. He died the night before last, we cremated him yesterday. He wanted to be cremated. But he left me something to give to you.'"

Red reached into his suit and produced Blinky Palermo's glasses. He solemnly presented the eyewear to the boss.

"That comes from when Julius Caesar was with the Mafia," a misty Natale said of the long-standing tradition. "That's from one man to another man, showing the respect for the man who's still alive: let him look through these glasses and see things the way I saw them."

Natale treasured the posthumous gift—until his wife lost the glasses in a mix-up with their cars. "I almost divorced her because of that. I'm not kidding. But let bygones be bygones, because I'm not Little Boy Blue over here, either."

He speaks the truth. Shortly after returning home, Natale—living large after his time in lockup—took up with a much younger blond mistress, a friend of his youngest daughter's named Ruthann Seccio. Natale spotted his future goomah sunbathing poolside in a bikini. Six months later, the two were a scandalous item, tooling around in Natale's white Eldorado with its blue leather seats.

Many in the mob were distressed by their boss's chasing a twentysomething Philly girl while his wife sat at home. It was unseemly.

Natale, looking back, doesn't disagree. "The life I led, especially when it came to marriage, wasn't right. I regret that—the only regret I have, you know? Ever hear that Sinatra song? 'Regrets, I've had a few. But too few to mention.'"

After the death of his friend Blinky, Natale returned to plotting the deaths of others. On May 29, 1996, video poker power broker Anthony "Tony Machines" Milicia was sitting behind the wheel of his Ford Explorer just a short block from one of his clients, Bonnie's Capistrano Bar. Milicia survived after taking a bullet to the back, and his face was cut by flying glass.

Milicia was shot after balking at Natale's demand for a cut of his weekly poker machine intake, which generated profits of close to $1 million a year. Once Milicia saw the light through the shattered glass of his car windows, all was forgiven. He and Natale subsequently met for drinks at a South Philadelphia bar.

"He wasn't a bad fella," said Natale. "I was glad he did survive."

Natale, in short and violent order, had restored some of the mob's old moneymaking cachet. Previte recalled that "every day was a different felony. I thought about nothing but making money from the minute I got up until the minute I went to bed."

That same year Natale spoke about his preferred method of handling mob problems. He advocated the beating of one mob associate " 'cause he answered me in a tone that he wasn't supposed to be doing."

Unfortunately, the conversation was captured by an FBI bug—and so were many more. On one, Natale ranted about the cowardly "rats" now so prevalent in his chosen field. "In life," he declared, "you have to do the right thing and be a man." His take on Atlantic City, long the family's crown jewel: "If we don't become successful in Atlantic City . . . we ought to put weights around our necks and jump in the river."

Even though Natale was paranoid about FBI ears, he couldn't stop himself from talking. Soon everyone would know everything there was to know about boss Ralph Natale.

26

By 1998, the Philly mob was lousy with rats and wiretaps as the FBI prepared to take down Natale and his crew. The feds were soon listening to Natale's every word about every aspect of the Philadelphia mob, tapping the racetrack restaurant along with his home telephone, his kitchen, his TV room, and the balcony of his Pennsauken, New Jersey, penthouse. A video camera was even installed at the track to collect images of the mobsters at work and play. Even worse, Previte used his new lease on life to wear a wire and record hundreds of conversations.

"Well, I was and I wasn't surprised by all the bugs," Natale reflected. "How much money they spent—they wired the whole racetrack, my phones, everything. How many millions of dollars they spent! And we talked about things. Assholes."

The word was soon out: indictments were on the way, and soon. Natale reached out to Merlino about the very uncertain future. "I told Joey, 'You do what you gotta do. Don't forget my wife.' And he said, 'Nah. Don't worry, Ralph.'"

Ralphy next sat down for a conversation with Lucia and

shared the bad news. His message to her was simple: "Listen, I don't know what the hell's coming down, they say a big indictment. Whatever. Don't worry about nothing. Joey and the crew made a commitment to me. They will bring over an envelope every month. So don't worry about it."

Natale never stopped fighting to protect what he had reclaimed. On March 18, 1998, Anthony Turra was shot in the right eye and the back by a killer in a ski mask and a black jacket. The sixty-one-year-old accused drug dealer was plotting to murder Merlino and seize Skinny Joey's gambling business—and even worse was caught doing so during a secretly recorded conversation with an FBI informant. One of his proposed methods of murder for Merlino: throwing hand grenades in Joey's house to "blow him from here to kingdom come."

The tape was played in open court. Turra—already fighting terminal cancer—went to the grave before a jury could render its verdict on his conspiracy and racketeering charges.

"There's a lot of people I saved from killing," said Natale. "Now, a guy wants to throw a grenade in your house—you can't let a guy talk that way. Joey came to me, and I said, 'Get it done.' There were certain things you can do, and certain things you can't. At least that's how I felt."

Natale went away before any indictments were returned, popped on a parole violation on June 11, 1998, and done in by his unapologetic embrace of his position atop the family. Though barred from contact with organized crime figures as part of his release, Natale was caught on surveillance on at least ten occasions consorting with his fellow mobsters. He had also ventured into Philadelphia without approval from his parole officer.

The arrest didn't come as a total surprise: One week

earlier, the courteous agents of the FBI told Natale and Skinny Joey they were captured on audio and video at a South Philly birthday party for the boss and his underboss. The two were also spied together in Cherry Hill at an unopened restaurant, and at the Greenhouse Restaurant in Margate, New Jersey.

Natale was leaving his home in the Cooper River Plaza South around 11:15 a.m. when he was greeted by four deputy US marshals and a Camden County sheriff's officer. Parole violations, unlike the typical arrest, require no court hearing. The boss was taken directly to jail, where he would remain until the state Parole Commission would hear his case.

Joey Merlino, in a stunning development unthinkable only a few years earlier, was now in line to become the street boss of the family.

Natale figured this was the tip of the iceberg. He was right: Previte alone had taped enough chatter to put everyone away for a long time.

Shortly after Merlino's birthday celebration, it was almost time to blow out the candles on the Natale era.

Natale, though off the streets, couldn't stay out of trouble. A week later his son-in-law was busted for running a methamphetamine ring and for possession of a .45-caliber automatic weapon. One year later, the Philly boss found himself indicted again on drug charges, accused of financing the operation. Previte's tapes offering the most damning evidence.

"My son-in-law, he was a carpenter, and at night he would make meth," Natale explained. "He said, 'I need some money.' Okay, here you go. They all knew I was putting the money up for it. They arrested him. Whatever."

And then one word of dismissal: "Amateurs."

Natale shrugged off the June 1999 indictment. "Why would it drive me crazy? Number one, every crime family in the country has drugs. That's bullshit that they don't. That's what started this thing. Lucky Luciano was the biggest pimp ever—white slavery, imagine that! And of course drugs. That happened. They all have it. Everybody's got a connection.

"It's all bullshit—'Don't do drugs, we'll kill you.' Well, go ahead and kill me. Don't do drugs? Everybody's doing drugs! Angelo Bruno's legitimate partner, Long John Martorano, was one of the biggest meth dealers in the city of Philadelphia. Also heroin early in his career. Ang knew that and still made him a legitimate partner."

The indictment actually came as a relief: the grand jury returned no homicide charges from the Philly mob war, and Natale knew Lucia would be taken care of this time. He had Joey Merlino's word.

"I get indicted, no money," he said, bile in his voice. "I thought a couple of murders were going to come up, too. Never happened. Joey Merlino told everybody, 'Don't worry about Ralph. He'll kill somebody in prison, and we'll never see him again, and that's that.'"

And so ended, after sixteen years of waiting and forty-five months as boss, the brief and ultimately bitter reign of Ralph Natale as the last true don of the Philadelphia family of La Cosa Nostra.

"I put the family back together," he said. "And I get arrested. Jesus Christ, what the frig happened? Then all hell breaks loose."

For a second time, Natale found his wife left adrift with no income as he wasted away behind bars. But this time, something inside him had changed. Skinny Joey was no Skinny Razor, and his crew were hardly worth comparing with the mafioso of Natale's youth. There was no Angelo Bruno, no John DiTullio, nor even a Salvie Testa in this motley crew of street thugs.

"Those punks, we made a pact in prison—if I get jammed up, you take care of my wife and family," Natale said. "And if you get jammed up, your girlfriend, your mother—I'll take care of them, and you know my record. Not a dime! I went away, not an envelope. I thought, 'Oh, yeah, I'm gonna see those punks in a courtroom.'"

When he was locked up yet again, Natale's rage against Merlino and the rest quickly reached a boiling point. The infuriated boss began to question his lifelong devotion to La Cosa Nostra. By now, the organization lived on only in the minds of men such as him. What was happening in the mob on the cusp of the new millennium had as much to do with the Mafia as the modern Olympics had to do with amateur athletics.

They were two different games entirely.

"So my wife and I reach out for Jimmy Maher, the head of the Philadelphia squad on organized crime," Natale remembered about a decision that once seemed unthinkable. "He was a young FBI guy when I got arrested in '79, but I didn't hold it against him, because he had to do his job. So now he stops by, he saw me, had a little conversation with me.

"I said, 'I'm thinking I might do something.' He knew— he said, 'They didn't do nothing for you, did they, Ralph?' I said, 'That's my business.' And eventually I decided I was going to do something against my nature. Those punks! I ain't gonna do no time for those punks! I wanna see them in the courtroom."

This was another of Natale's pinpoints in time, when a single choice transforms a man's life: the lifelong gangster turned his back on the life that had meant everything to him since he was a boy and became a federal witness.

Joey Merlino had finally accomplished what the Philadelphia authorities, the FBI, and the US Congress could not. After decades of silence, Ralph Natale was ready to speak inside a courtroom about the inner workings of La Cosa Nostra. Natale was quickly dubbed King Rat.

But the old gangster bristles at the suggestion that he was an informant. "I became a government witness. I never wrote a wire. I never entrapped anybody. I didn't inform on nobody."

On May 5, 2000, the former Philadelphia family boss arrived at the Camden federal courthouse to confess all in his lifetime of crime. His plane from prison was fogged in, and Natale's charcoal suit arrived two hours before he did. He then pleaded guilty to seven killings, five attempted murders, extortion, gambling, and drug dealing. Lucia was waiting for him, along with son Frank.

It took just one hour to erase five decades of mob life, putting Ralph Natale on the side of the federal government. The *Philadelphia Daily News* noted that Natale, facing life in prison, was "expected to do far less time in jail."

Natale, before his courthouse reunion with Merlino, would first see the mayor of Camden, Milton Milan. The two had struck up a crooked business relationship, with Milan indicted and Natale called to the witness stand.

"Milton Milan would take anything—even a hot stove," Natale recalled of the corrupt politician. "He was what the guys in Chicago called double-breasted, meaning he had a wife and kids, and a girlfriend/mistress and another whole life. Oh, my! You're gonna have trouble. We were introduced, and we talked and became friends."

Natale offered a deal where both sides would profit from millions of dollars in state and federal funds earmarked for Camden's redevelopment. The mob boss, after reading about the potential windfall in the newspaper, approached Milan to offer the services of his new construction company—which would use minority-owned businesses as a front. The mobster then sweetened the pot with an immediate cash dividend.

"I brought out an envelope with five Ben Franklins inside, handed it to him, and said, 'Have a good time tonight.' He said, 'No, no'—and then right into his pocket."

There was more money to come, as much as $50,000 funneled to the corrupt mayor. Natale recalled paying for Milan and his mistress to take a 1998 vacation in sunny Florida.

Natale first took the stand as a federal witness in 2000. Turning his back on the mob to take the witness stand against Milan, he said, was as easy as slipping out of his prison duds into one of the tailored suits he wore to court during four days of testimony. "It didn't bother me a bit. The thing I did when I got home to straighten things out—I had to do this, that, the mayor. It didn't bother me. And then it was part of my deal. It didn't bother me. I didn't have anything to prove. What did the mayor end up doing? Three, four years?"

It turned out to be five years of a seven-year jail term.

From the witness stand, Natale offered a pithy summation of his relationship with Milan: "I wanted him to rely on me, and nobody else. If he had a headache, I would send him an aspirin."

The mayor was convicted on fourteen of the nineteen federal counts against him.

Natale's cooperation helped convict two Milan coconspirators, politician James Mathes and former union boss Daniel Daidone. The latter was Natale's bagman, delivering payoffs to Milan.

The main event was next, with Skinny Joey and the rest. This time, Natale's testimony reflected both federal agreement and personal animus: "I couldn't wait to see Mr. Merlino again in person."

Natale, impeccably dressed, climbed into the witness stand on March 30, 2001, the highest-ranking member of the American Mafia ever to testify against his mob compatriots. He wore a dark blue business suit, neatly tailored, along with a white shirt and a blue tie. Merlino fired a death stare at his old boss when Natale swore to tell the truth, the whole truth, and nothing but the truth.

Skinny Joey was on trial with six codefendants in a massive racketeering case with charges of murder, attempted murder, extortion, gambling, and dealing in stolen property. Star witness Natale was expected to link Merlino to the dead bodies cited in the sprawling indictment.

After years of waiting to look Merlino in the face one more time, Natale felt strangely empty as he began a long recitation of his life in crime. He spent fourteen days on the witness stand in Philadelphia federal court. "I felt nothing. Nothing at all. I'm a cold fish when it comes to that. I'm looking at punks. If it was men, and I did something like that, I couldn't do that. They're punks! Look at them! They didn't take care of my wife and family. You pieces of shit! A man's gotta take care of that, I don't justify nothing. I know why I did what I did."

Which is not to say Natale was a dispassionate witness. He glared right back at Merlino, their eyes locked in an uncomfortable stare down that lasted until a federal prosecutor broke the tension.

Natale offered a one-fingered salute—fuck you, Joey—to his old charges as they shared the courtroom. "I challenged all of them. He must have made a face or something. He's such a punk, and afraid of me. Of course, I looked right at him. I called him a punk at every trial I was in. I put my life up for him in that cell at McKean. He didn't bother me. I've been in trouble since the day I came out of my mother's womb."

Natale recounted his long-ago murders of Feeney and McGreal and offered details on other mob rubouts during his brief and bloody reign. A defense lawyer asked Natale about reports that his family was threatened. The former boss was caught on taped phone calls from prison announcing his imminent return to Philly—a declaration that, though bogus, would deliver a message to his old mob colleagues.

Natale offered his own translation years later: "Whatever I do, don't you touch my family. 'Cause you won't have no family when I get home, if I do come home."

During his fourteen days on the witness stand, he appeared briefly before the very man who wore a wire against him: Previte, aka the Fat Rat. The two, perhaps fortunately, never crossed paths during their time working for the feds.

"I didn't even know he was there," said Natale of his mob bête noire. Previte testified that Merlino had borrowed money from Natale, gone to Las Vegas, and blown the whole stake.

Natale acknowledges that even while in the embrace of the FBI and federal prosecutors, he was plotting to whack archenemy Merlino. "Positively! What am I gonna do? That's me. I'm never gonna change until the day I die. He owed me money. They all owed me money. That's the way I lived my life."

The jury returned on July 20, 2001—and acquitted Merlino and his associates of the murders and attempted murders after a four-month trial. They were convicted on lesser counts of racketeering and racketeering conspiracy, including gambling and extortion.

Eleven of the twelve jurors believed the defendants were guilty but thought the government had failed to prove its case.

"There was enough gray area," one juror explained to *The Philadelphia Inquirer*. "We believed they did it . . . but we couldn't convict on a belief."

Natale, despite his lingering animus toward Merlino and the rest, insists the verdict meant nothing to him. "I'm gonna tell you something: I wasn't disappointed. That may sound funny, but it's true. I was obligated to talk, and I kept my obligation. I wouldn't want anybody to go to prison. I would have rather done what I had to do on the street. I had no love for them punks. But I know what prison can do to a man. I would have rather taken care of business myself."

A few months after the Merlino acquittal, Natale learned that payback had finally come to Long John Martorano for his alliance with Nicky Scarfo. The old schemer died on February 5, 2002, three weeks after two shooters unloaded on him while he was behind the wheel of his Lincoln Continental.

He had returned to Philly three years earlier after doing seventeen years for the McCullough murder and a drug rap.

Natale was called in 2004 to testify at a second trial for Merlino, this time for the Sodano execution. Although acquitted of the charge in the earlier racketeering case, a federal judge ruled there was no double jeopardy in a second trial with murder as the charge. Natale arrived at the Newark federal courthouse feeling this case didn't have a chance after learning that prosecutors would not call Sodano's killer, Philly Fay Casale, who had joined Natale on the side of the government.

"They said he was half-crazy," Natale said. "But they didn't bring the shooter to court! If I knew he wasn't testifying, I wouldn't have even gone up there. Philly Fay and I were cellmates in [New Jersey prison] Fairton. We had a great time. I mean, he was a killer—but what a great guy. Sometimes you gotta do what you gotta do."

Natale arrived for his federal witness finale in February 2004 appearing far more subdued than in his first three trips to the witness stand. His goatee was considerably grayer, and his pricey suits had been replaced by prison-issued shirt and pants. He told the same basic story as the first time, with the same basic result: Skinny Joey walked.

The two frenemies would never see each other again.

27

THE BIG PAYBACK

Natale's deal with the government did not come with a get-out-of-jail-free card. He remained behind bars while appearing at four separate trials in four years, knowing all along that his ultimate fate belonged to a federal judge.

There was one problem: when Natale arrived in Camden federal court for sentencing in January 2005, the cooperating witness found a most uncooperative judge.

Natale was facing a possible life sentence in his plea agreement, but expected a much better deal. Recent history was on his side: Gambino family turncoat Sammy "the Bull" Gravano admitted nineteen murders and received just five years. Scarfo's traitorous nephew Philip "Crazy Phil" Leonetti was sentenced to the same amount of time after copping to his own murderous exploits: a trail of ten bodies.

Five years sounded about right to Ralphy, and he'd already been locked up since 1998. "Time served would let me walk out of court as a free man," he thought.

US District Court judge Joseph E. Irenas was unimpressed by Natale's turnaround, by the account of FBI agents and federal prosecutors hailing by his efforts, by the presence of Lucia and a dozen of her children and grandchildren sitting in the courtroom.

Natale, his voice cracking and tears filling his eyes, stood and made his own plea: "I can't bring anything back. I go to sleep every night with the shame and remorse that I feel . . . and I wake up with it."

Every word fell on deaf ears. The hearing lasted four hours. The optimistic Natale's hopes for a happy ending waned with each tick of the clock. And then Irenas spoke.

"The judge said, 'This is not gonna be another Gravano or Leonetti thing,'" recalled Ralph. "I said, 'Oh, man—here we go.' Unreal. Everybody thought I'd be able to walk out—I had almost five years in already. I felt bad for my family. But he took so long, I knew I was in trouble. But that was then. This is now. And that's what counts."

Irenas banged Natale with thirteen years in prison on his guilty pleas to drug dealing, racketeering, and corruption charges.

"The judge sentenced me not for what I pleaded to, but for what he was told I did," Natale said. "He thought I was Genghis Khan! He gave me as much time as the guys I testified against. He wanted me to die in prison. He wanted to hurt me."

Despite the harsh sentence, Natale could see a day when all this was behind him, when he would return home to Lucia and the kids and the grandkids. "I had complete faith that I was gonna live until I want to die," he said with a chuckle. "If I spent my time thinking about when I was going to die, I wouldn't be Ralph Natale."

If he was lucky, Ralph faced another six years in federal lockup. He headed back to prison in Allenwood, Pennsylvania.

Upon arrival, he was greeted by Anthony "Tony the Barber" Angelo, a onetime hit man for the Chicago mob. The ex-marine and Purple Heart recipient from the Korean War was doing life, leaving Natale to reflect on the circumstances that had brought them together in this place.

"You say, 'Why do guys become what we are?'" he mused. "Every different reason—this way, that way."

Angelo—his nickname came from his day job as a haircutter—served as Ralph's hype man, spreading the gospel of Natale.

"When I went there, all the guys who didn't know me had heard of me—some of the black guys, the Latinos, they said, 'He was a boss, wasn't he?'" Natale said. "You know what Tony said? 'He wasn't a boss. He was a don. He was the last of the dons. There's nobody else. He worked his way up. He wasn't handed it.'"

His Allenwood arrival caused a stir among the prison's mobbed-up population. Natale was greeted with sweat suits and his beloved cigars. "It's a tradition," he explained.

Natale made another new friend in Allenwood: an Irish priest from New York who made the trip to Pennsylvania, where he tended an imprisoned flock of about seventy Catholics. He worked on Wall Street before answering his calling as a man of the cloth. The unlikely pals quickly hit it off, sharing cigars after mass and griping about the lack of good Italian food.

"He was a real man, this guy—smoked, laughed, cursed once in a while," said Natale. "He would come up, he'd serve Communion, and he'd hear confession. And I hadn't gone to confession for forty-five years—before somebody's wedding. It wasn't mine! I asked him, 'Father McDevitt, could you do me a favor after mass one Sunday?'

"He said, 'Yeah, what is it, Ralphy? Of course.'

"I said, 'Would you hear my confession next week?' He said it would be an honor. And he did, he heard my confession. I was the last one in that day."

The mob killer and the man of God sat face-to-face inside a federal prison as Natale recounted his sins, his darkest secrets from a life of murder and mob mayhem.

"After we finished, we went out for a smoke. I had my cigar. And he told me, 'You know, this made me feel glad that I'm a priest, because you chose me to hear your confession.'

"And I told him, 'Because you're a man, and a man of the cloth, I know you believe in what you're talking about. A lot of them don't.' We shook hands and hugged one another. It was like nothing because I trusted him. No bullshit, no nothing. It felt good telling him. He was such a good guy. I know that's what a priest should be like."

Getting old in federal lockup came with its own set of woes. Natale remembers a killer toothache that left him in agony for three weeks, with no way of seeing a dentist. "To get a dentist in Allenwood, you had to be the president. Finally, I said the hell with this. I got the dental floss and turned my back from the cell window. I thought, 'I gotta pull this—now.' I worked the dental floss down, cut into the gum, and pop! It popped right out. All the blood came out. Tony the Barber stole a bottle of peroxide for me, and I washed my mouth out."

Natale's smile on the day of his release was hardly as bright as the one he brought into Allenwood. The feds offered to put him in the Witness Protection Program, but he quickly refused after leaving prison for the last time on May 19, 2011.

"I never went to no program," he said with pride. "They said, 'We'll put you in the best place.' What? Come on! My family, my children, my grandchildren—I can't see them? No way. I didn't become a witness to live in some closet in Omaha, Nebraska."

Natale proved right about one thing: he wound up doing more time than his nemesis Merlino. Skinny Joey walked out of a Florida prison two months before Natale's release.

Once released, Natale made it clear to one and all that he was done as a witness. He'd gone toe to toe with Merlino and the rest. Natale was done working for the government. "Even now, to this day, they want this or that. And I told them when I got done, I will never be a witness against anybody for the rest of my life, and you remember that. I told all the agents and the US attorney. Two years ago, they took a ride to see me when I was living in Baltimore—two FBI agents. They asked about a name.

"I said, 'Nah. I don't know. Remember what I told you when I came home? I'll never be a witness again.'"

When Natale exited prison for the last time, his loyal wife, Lucia, and their three daughters were waiting outside. "And then," he said simply, "I came home."

EPILOGUE:

The don, in his dotage, steers well clear of the streets of Philadelphia and his checkered past. When he talks about the family, he's referring to the ever-expanding Natale clan.

He's now the patriarch of a large, sprawling, and successful clan that stretches across four generations. Natale speaks fondly of his wife, and proudly of their five kids, their grandkids, and great-grandkids. The streets of Philadelphia are a thing of the past, replaced by wandering deer and wild turkeys. Many nights, Natale sleeps on the couch—it's the one place in his new home that feels like a prison bed, and it helps him to drift off.

The only gun he wields is a water pistol to chase the cat off the living room furniture.

Natale is just as surprised as anyone—and more than most—that he's still alive and well.

"I mean, they were betting I wouldn't make twenty-five years old when I was on the street," he says, enjoying the life of a contented man. "He'll never make it! Now they're dead, and I'm here. It's tough."

He laughs.

Natale mourns the loss of the old Mafia, the world where he grew up. The whole thing was killed by men who were never satisfied with their position or their riches, men without respect for the Life or their own lives.

"Greed destroyed everything," he declares. "Everything. Ever watch that movie *The Wolf of Wall Street*? There's greed in everything—in Wall Street, in politics, in the mob. I can't make head or tails about it. If you're doing okay, why get greedy? Why go overboard? You're making a living, taking care of your wife and family.

"You've got a few extra dollars to gamble and have a good time with. What do you need more for?"

Reflecting on his decades in the mob, Natale recalls his personal highlight: "When Carlo and Ang made me and sent me out with all the power of their two families."

The flip side, his lowest moment? "When I was in prison," he replies quickly, "and they killed Angelo Bruno."

Natale, like his old pal Blinky Palermo, wants his remains cremated. He's already decided on an epitaph: HERE LIES A FOOL.

"I mean that," he says seriously. "That's what I have to say. Put that on my gravestone. That's what we all are, men like me."

But that's somewhere in the future. Right now, he's too busy to consider that option: "I can't drop dead. I got too much to do in my life." And while the past may be the past, that's the world where Ralph Natale finds that he still often lives.

"My head is like an attic in an old house," he finally says. "It's filled with all sorts of things. I think about it constantly. Even when I'm asleep.

"The last dream is that I'm in prison again. Every night."

POSTSCRIPT

On Aug, 4, 2016, Manhattan Federal Prosecutor Preet Bharara unsealed a lengthy mob indictment against members of four New York organized crime families—Bonanno, Luchese, Gambino and Genovese—and the remnants of the old Philadelphia mob.

Among the obscure Mafiosi arrested were goodfellas known on the street as Tony the Wig, Mustache Pat, Tugboat, Stymie and Harpo. Only one name jumped off the 32 pages detailing the myriad crimes: Joseph "Skinny Joey" Merlino, busted again on a federal racketeering charge, unable to get out of his own way.

"I wasn't that surprised," said Natale about the arrest. "I expected it. It's a wonder somebody didn't put two bullets into him since he got out."

The now 54-year-old Merlino, as recently as three years earlier, had sworn off the mob life. "I want no part of that. Too many rats," he told veteran Philadelphia mob chronicler George Anastasia. After serving 11 years in prison on his federal raps, Ralph's old nemesis relocated to south

Florida and opened a restaurant named "Merlino's"—where he served as the maître d'. The place suffered through financial woes, in part because Merlino was jailed for four months in 2015 after the feds spied him inside a Florida cigar bar with fellow Philly ex-pat Johnny Ciancaglini. His latest arrest left its future uncertain.

Merlino, it seems, couldn't escape the lure and allure of the old days, when he served as Natale's underboss as they reclaimed the city after the disastrous reign of Nicky Scarfo. It's the old definition of insanity: Doing the exact same thing over and over—and expecting a different result.

"Look, his IQ might be 84," said Natale of Merlino. "He's a complete idiot. He put himself in this position. If he goes away this time, it's going to destroy him. When he went away before, he did time as the boss—he was young, and thinking about coming home, and people think about you differently."

If convicted this time, Merlino could stay behind bars into his seventies. He was accused as one of the organization's ruling triumvirate, along with a pair of Genovese family capos.

The idea of Merlino running the Philadelphia mob from Boca Raton seemed a stretch—like Marlins manager Don Mattingly running the Yankees from Miami. There's even some question as to its current membership and activities, as the indictment listed six other Floridians as defendants, but not a single resident of the city of Brotherly Love. Yet court papers indicated "the case against Merlino is extremely strong, consisting, in part, of numerous explicit recordings in which Merlino discussed the crimes that he was committing and exhibited his role as a leader."

Federal investigators say Merlino had failed to listen to

his own advice about informants. An undercover FBI agent and a cooperating witness managed to infiltrate the mob consortium dubbed by prosecutors as "The East Coast La Cosa Nostra Enterprise," operating from Massachusetts to Florida. The witness, according to prosecutors, worked directly under Merlino at one point during the probe.

The details aren't important to Natale. The bottom line for the retired gangster: The mob of his youth is as dead as Angelo Bruno or Salvie Testa.

"They are what they are," he said of the 21st century mob. "I'm not patting myself on the back here, but I come from a different time and a different place. There are no old-timers, no men running things. The intelligence quotient is way down.

"Believe me, I'm in a better place."

INDEX

Accardo, Anthony for
     Chicago, 5–6, 53
  Congress against, 161
  FBI against, 100
accountability, 23
Aldrich, Fred, 203
Ali, Muhammad, 42, 44–47
Allen, Charlie, xiii, 204–5
  betrayal by, 97–99, 163
  as bodyguard, 69
  for drugs, 96–97
  for FBI, 97
  in mafia, 8, 71–75
  Ralph and, 8, 165
Amuso, Vic, 199–200
Anastasia, Albert, 33
Anastasia, George, 236
Angelo, Anthony ("Tony the
     Barber"), 231–32
arson
  against Mr. Living Room,
     94–96
  by Ralph, 95–96
Atlantic City
  casinos in, 51–53, 57, 88–90
  for La Cosa Nostra, 216

Johnson in, 51
Local 54 for, 134, 136, 139, 145,
     195
  for mafia, 7–8, 51–64, 134, 138
Avena, John, 32

Baldino, Richard ("Bucky"), 62
Balistrieri, Frank ("Mr. Big"), 55
bar tending
  Local 170 for, 52–53
  for Ralph, 79
Barone, Joe "Pep," 43
Barry, Harry, 25–27
baseball, 14, 19–20
Bernard, Raymond, xiii, 207
  betrayal by, 97–99
  for drugs, 96–97
  for FBI, 97
betrayal. See also Federal Bureau of
     Investigation
  by Allen, 97–99, 163
  by Bernard, 97–99
  by Bocchino, 106–8, 113,
     179–82
  against Bruno, A., 103–9
  by Caponigro, 102–9, 112–14

betrayal (*continued*)
by Casale, 228
by Casella, 144–49
by DiPretoro, 172–73
by Ferrante, 106–8, 113
by Gambino, J., 179–82
by Lansky, 43
by Martorano, R., 150–54
against McCullough, 136–40
against Merlino, J., 225–27,
237–38
against Milan, 223–25
by Narducci, F., 145–49
against Palermo, 107
by Previte, 216, 218–20, 226
against Ralph, 97–99, 216–20
by Ralph, 222–28
Ralph discussing, 106–8, 152, 160
by Salerno, 104, 106, 108,
112–13
against Scarfo, N., 147
by Scarfo, N., 116, 133–40
by Sindone, 102, 108–9, 110–13
against Stanfa, John, 203–4
by Stanfa, John, 102, 108–9,
111–14, 131–32, 179–82
against Testa, P., 116, 146–48
by Turchi, 196–97
Bharara, Preet, 236
Bianculli, Edward, 173
Billy Duke's, 66
Bilotti, Tommy, 145–46
Black Mafia, 40, 157, 207
Blue Ribbon Meats, 87
Boardwalk Empire, 51
Bocchino, Felix ("Little Felix")
betrayal by, 106–8, 113, 179–82
murder of, 198
bodyguards
Allen as, 69
DeMaio as, 127
Gatti as, 36–37
Bonanno family. *See* New York
City

Bouras, Stevie
as hit man, 152
murder of, 151–54
boxing
Ali for, 42, 44–47
Barone in, 43
Carbo in, 43–44, 46
Jordan in, 44
LaMotta in, 43
Liston for, 42–47
mafia and, 42–47
Palermo in, 43–44, 47
Patterson for, 42
Williams in, 43
Bruno, Angelo ("The Docile
Don"), xi
betrayal against, 103–9
Caponigro and, 41, 112–14
Castellano and, 87–88
for La Cosa Nostra, 35–36,
72–79, 83–84, 91–93, 134
DiTullio and, 36–39
FBI against, 99–100
as friend, to Ralph, 68–69,
117–19
Gambino, C., and, 29–30, 33,
35–36, 51–54, 70
Kossman and, 110
mafia ascension for, 32–41
as mentor, for Ralph, 5–6, 8, 22,
28–31, 39, 49, 53–54, 60, 112
murder of, 110–14
pornography and, 48–49
Ralph discussing, 162–65
Stanfa, John and, 92–93,
108–9
Testa, P., for, 39–41, 77–78, 111
wake for, 120–23
Bruno, Sue, 84, 91–92, 110, 112,
120–22
Bruno wake
Leonetti at, 122
Merlino, J., at, 122
Merlino, S., at, 122

Scarfo, N., at, 122
Scarfo, N., Jr., at, 122
Testa, P., at, 122
Testa, S., at, 122
Buchalter, Louis ("Lepke"), 61–62
Budweiser Bar, 15
Bufalino, Russell, 77–78
Byrne, Brendan, 88

Cadillac Linen Co., 61
Capone, Al, 21
Caponigro, Anthony ("Tony
    Bananas"), xiii
  betrayal by, 102–9, 112–14
  Bruno, A., and, 41, 112–14
  Down Neck for, 106
  as hit man, 112–14
  in mafia, 88–90
  murder of, 125–28
Caprio, Peter ("Pete the Crumb"),
    214
Caramandi, Nicholas ("Nicky the
    Crow"), 172, 177
Carbo, Frankie
  in boxing, 43–44, 46
  as hit man, 43
  in mafia, 43–44, 46
  prison for, 44
Casale, Philip ("Philly Fay"), 214,
    228
Casella, Pete, xiii
  betrayal by, 144–49
  DiTullio compared to, 141
  in mafia, 141–42, 171
casinos
  in Atlantic City, 51–53, 57,
    88–90
  Dante for, 33–34
  Local 54 for, 134, 136, 139, 145,
    195
  for mafia, 51–53, 88–90
  Ralph for, 52–54
  unions for, 8, 134, 136, 139, 145,
    195

Castellano, Paul
  Bruno, A., and, 87–88
  in mafia, 86–88, 116
  murder of, 178
  for New York City, 135–36
chauffeurs. See drivers
Chicago
  Accardo for, 5–6, 53
  Capone for, 21
  for mafia, 5–6, 52–53
  Ralph in, 55–56
childhood, 11–17, 155–56
Ciancaglini, John, 213, 237
Ciancaglini, Joseph ("Chickie"),
    180
  in mafia, 129–31, 192–93
  murder attempt on, 201–2
Ciancaglini, Michael ("Mikey
    Chang"), xii
  as hit man, 197–98
  in mafia, 181–82, 200–201
  murder of, 202–3
  Ralph and, 192–97
Cifelli, Michael ("Mikey Coco"),
    168–69
Clay, Cassius. See Ali, Muhammad
Congress, US
  against Accardo, 161
  against Hanley, 161
  Merlino, J., and, 165–66
  Ralph and, 160–66
  Roth for, 162–64
  Rudman for, 162–64
  Scarfo, N., and, 161, 165
Conte, Rick, 76–79
Corona di Ferra, 34
La Cosa Nostra. See also mafia
  Atlantic City for, 216
  Bruno, A., for, 35–36, 72–79,
    83–84, 91–93, 134
  DiTullio for, 21–24, 45–46, 54
  in Florida, 237–38
  induction for, 90, 143–44
  meeting for, 209–11

La Cosa Nostra (*continued*)
  Merlino, J., for, 219–21
  Milan and, 223–25
  Ralph and, 5, 180–81, 208–17,
    221–22
  Scarfo, N., for, 150–51, 171,
    178–79, 187
  Testa, P., for, 129–30, 133,
    135–40, 141–43
  Testa, S. for, 175
  unions for, 71
Currier & Ives Restaurant, 208
Curro, Jeanette, 152–53

Daidone, Daniel, 225
Dangerous Special Offender Act,
  100–101
Dante, Ignazio
  for casinos, 33–34
  as hit man, 33–35
DelGiorno, Tommy, 177
Dellacroce, Aniello ("Mr. Neil"),
  70, 86
DeLuca, ("Louie Irish"), 196–97
DeMaio, Vinnie, 127
DeRose, Charlie, 118
DiAddorio, James ("Jimmy
  Broom"), 198–99
DiBernardo, Robert, 48–50
DiPretoro, Teddy
  betrayal by, 172–73
  as hit man, 147–48, 173
  in mafia, 144–45
DiTullio, John ("Skinny Razor"), xi
  Bruno, A., and, 36–39
  Casella compared to, 141
  for La Cosa Nostra, 21–24,
    45–46, 54
  death of, 68
  as friend of Ralph, 25
  as hit man, 38
  in mafia, 26–27, 32–33
domestic violence, 13–14
Down Neck (bar), 106

drivers
  Aldrich as, 203
  Ralph as, 28–31
  Salerno as, 104, 106, 108, 112–13
  Stanfa, John as, 111–14
  Vadino as, 44, 62–63, 72–73
Drug Enforcement Agency, 97–98
drugs
  Allen for, 96–97
  Bernard for, 96–97
  Ralph and, 96–97, 221–22

Eckstine, Billy, 25

family. *See also* marriage
  of Ralph, 117–18, 120–24,
    155–57, 161–62, 218–19,
    234–35
  relatives as, 6, 11–15, 19–22,
    24–25
Federal Bureau of Investigation
  (FBI)
  against Accardo, 100
  Allen for, 97
  Bernard for, 97
  against Bruno, A., 99–100
  Caprio for, 214
  Caramandi for, 172, 177
  Casale for, 228
  DelGiorno for, 177
  against Gambino, C., 100
  Leonetti for, 179–80
  against mafia, 45, 127
  against Martorano, R., 118
  Natale, L., and, 98
  Pistone for, 204
  Previte for, 216, 218–20, 226
  against Ralph, 99–100, 216–20
  Ralph for, 222–28
  against Stanfa, John, 131–32
Ferrante, Tony ("Meats"), 106–8,
  113
Ferrara Bakery and Café, 51–52
Fitzgerald, Ella, 25

Fitzsimmons, Frank, 80–81, 83
Florida. *See also* prison
    La Cosa Nostra in, 237–38
    Ralph in, 96–98
food, for Ralph, 99
Freeney, George, 65–67
The Friendly Tavern
    in Philadelphia, 22–23, 26,
        36–38
    for Ralph, 22–23
friendship, 25, 68–69, 117–19

Gambino, Carlo
    Bruno, A., and, 29–30, 33,
        35–36, 51–54, 70
    death of, 86–87
    FBI against, 100
    pornography and, 48–50
    Ralph and, 52–54
    Stanfa, John for, 92
Gambino, John
    betrayal by, 179–82
    in mafia, 131, 178
Gambino family. *See* New York
    City
gambling. *See* casinos
gangs, for bikers, 48–49
Garden State Race Track, 72, 76,
    208, 214, 218
Gatti, Lefty, 36–37
Genovese family. *See* New York
    City
George Washington Elementary
    School, 27
Gerace, Frank, 134, 136–39
Gigante, Vforcent "the Chfor"
    mafia ascension for, 104–5
Gigante, Vincent "the Chin," 57
    in mafia, 126, 171
Giovanelli, Federico ("Fritzy"),
    207
Gotti, John
    mafia ascension for, 178–79
    McGreal and, 69–70

for New York City, 30, 50,
    199–200
in prison, 69–70
Grande, Salvatore ("Wayne")
    discussing Ralph, 76
    as hit man, 176
    induction for, 143
Gravano, Sammy ("the Bull")
    as hit man, 128–29
    in prison, 229–30
Greek mafia, 151
Greeley, John, 81–82

Half-Hour Club, 65
Hanley, Ed
    Congress against, 161
    for unions, 5–6, 58, 139, 206–7
hit men. *See also* murder
    Bouras as, 152
    Caponigro as, 112–14
    Carbo as, 43
    Ciancaglini, John as, 213
    Ciancaglini, M. as, 197–98
    Conte as, 76–79
    Dante as, 33–35
    DiPretoro as, 147–48, 173
    DiTullio, 38
    Grande as, 176
    Gravano as, 128–29
    Marinucci as, 147–48
    Martorano, G. as, 153–54
    Martorano, R., as, 140
    Merlino, S. as, 168–69
    Pungitore, J., as, 172, 175–76
    Ralph as, 1–3, 7–9, 49, 66–67,
        74–76, 96
    Scarfo, N., as, 133–34
    Testa, P., as, 39–40
    Testa, S. as, 168–69, 171–74
Hoffa, Jimmy
    in prison, 80
    Ralph and, 58–60, 80–85
    for unions, 6–7, 58–61, 80–85
Hoffman, Cappy, 62–64

Hotel Employees and Restaurant Employees International Union. *See* Local 170

Ida, Joe, 33–35
Iezzi, Freddie, 23–24, 35–37, 39–40
induction
  for La Cosa Nostra, 90, 143–44
  for Grande, 143
  for Leonetti, 143
  for Merlino, J., 212
  for Narducci, F., Jr., 143
  for Pungitore, A., 143
  for Ralph, 54, 212
  for Testa, S., 143–44
International Brotherhood of Teamsters, 80
Irenas, Joseph E., 229–30
Irish Republican Army, 147–48
Italian Market, 17, 23, 39–40

Jewish mafia, 61–64
Johnson, Enoch ("Nucky"), 51
Jordan, Don, 44

killing. *See* murder
Kossman, Jacob, 78
  Bruno, A., and, 110
  for Ralph, 101

LaMotta, Jake, 43
Lansky, Meyer, 43
Lanzilotti, Leon ("Yonnie"), 204
Latin Casino (club), 61
Leonetti, Phil, 138
  at Bruno wake, 122
  for FBI, 179–80
  induction for, 143
  in mafia, 115, 149–50
  prison for, 229–30
Lewisburg. *See* prison
Liston, Charles ("Sonny"), 42–47
loan sharking, 94–96

Local 54, 134, 136, 139, 145, 195
Local 170, 134
  for bar tending, 52–53
  DeRose for, 118
  for mafia, 2, 55–56, 60–61, 70
  McGreal for, 70
  Ralph for, 52–53, 57
  Rifkin for, 61–63
  Siedman for, 61–63
Luchese family. *See* New York City
Luciano, Charles ("Lucky"), 29
Lucibello, Gaeton, 202

made men. *See* induction
mafia. *See also* betrayal; bodyguards; Bruno, Angelo; La Cosa Nostra; drivers; hit men; induction; Merlino, Joseph; murder
  Allen in, 8, 71–75
  Amuso in, 199–200
  Atlantic City for, 7–8, 51–64, 134, 138
  Balistrieri in, 55
  Barone in, 43
  biker gangs and, 48–49
  Bilotti in, 145–46
  Black Mafia as, 40, 157, 207
  boxing and, 42–47
  Bruno, S., and, 120–22
  Buchalter in, 61–62
  Capone in, 21
  Caponigro in, 88–90
  Carbo in, 43–44, 46
  Casella in, 141–42, 171
  casinos for, 51–53, 88–90
  Castellano in, 86–88, 116
  Chicago for, 5–6, 52–53
  Ciancaglini, Joseph, in, 129–31, 192–93
  Ciancaglini, M., in, 181–82, 200–201
  Currier & Ives Restaurant for, 208

Dellacroce in, 70, 86
DiPretoro in, 144–45
DiTullio in, 26–27, 32–33
Down Neck for, 106
FBI against, 45, 127
Gambino, J., in, 131, 178
Gigante in, 126, 171
for Greeks, 151
Hoffman in, 62–64
Ida in, 33–35
Iezzi in, 23–24, 35–37, 39–40
for Jews, 61–64
Leonetti in, 115, 149–50
Liston and, 42–47
Local 170 for, 2, 55–56, 60–61, 70
Manna in, 115–16, 136, 149–50,
  171
Marinucci in, 144–45
Marrone in, 77, 81
Martorano, R., in, 49, 91,
  117–19, 123–24
Merlino, S., in, 114–15, 144, 176
Monte in, 129–30
Murder Inc., as, 61–63
Mustache Petes as, 23
Narducci, F., in, 141–42
Natale, L., and, 120–24, 218–19
Natale, "Spike" in, 12–15,
  20–22, 155–56
in New Jersey, 8, 30, 35, 88–90
in New York City, 28–31, 33,
  35–36, 49, 86–90, 145–46,
  213
in The New York Times, 203–4
O'Neill and, 58
Palermo in, 43–44, 47, 69,
  71–72
in Philadelphia, 5–8, 32–33,
  203–4
pornography and, 48–50
Previte in, 8
Ralph discussing, 9, 14–16,
  54–55, 82, 103–4, 125,
  130–31, 138, 140, 142, 148,

176, 191–93, 203, 216–17, 235,
  238
Rastelli in, 124
Reginelli in, 26
retirement in, 34
Rickshaw Inn for, 79, 81–84
Salerno in, 81, 88–90
Scarfo, N., in, 8, 114–15,
  129–30, 168–69
Sindone in, 93
Stanfa, John in, 91–93
Testa, P., in, 17, 114–15
Testa, S., in, 114
Tieri in, 104–6, 125, 127–28
Torano's Italian Bar and
  Restaurant for, 110–12
Triangle Civic Improvement
  Association for, 104–5
Turchi in, 77, 81
Verna in, 116–17
Virgilio in, 115, 136
Waldorf Astoria Hotel for,
  29–30, 35
in The Wall Street Journal, 167
Wallace in, 14–15
Weisberg in, 62–64
Young Turks as, 23
mafia ascension
  for Bruno, A., 32–41
  for Gigante, 104–5
  for Gotti, 178–79
  for Ralph, 19–25, 52–55, 68,
    189–90, 196–205
  for Scarfo, N., 116, 149–51
  for Stanfa, John, 200–204
  for Testa, S., 167–71
mafia ceremony. See induct
Manhattan. See New Yor′
Manna, Bobby, 115–16
  149–50, 171
Manni, Jack, 188
Mantle, Mickey, ′
Marinucci, Roc
  as hit man,

Dellacroce in, 70, 86
DiPretoro in, 144–45
DiTullio in, 26–27, 32–33
Down Neck for, 106
FBI against, 45, 127
Gambino, J., in, 131, 178
Gigante in, 126, 171
for Greeks, 151
Hoffman in, 62–64
Ida in, 33–35
Iezzi in, 23–24, 35–37, 39–40
for Jews, 61–64
Leonetti in, 115, 149–50
Liston and, 42–47
Local 170 for, 2, 55–56, 60–61, 70
Manna in, 115–16, 136, 149–50,
171
Marinucci in, 144–45
Marrone in, 77, 81
Martorano, R., in, 49, 91,
117–19, 123–24
Merlino, S., in, 114–15, 144, 176
Monte in, 129–30
Murder Inc., as, 61–63
Mustache Petes as, 23
Narducci, F., in, 141–42
Natale, L., and, 120–24, 218–19
Natale, "Spike" in, 12–15,
20–22, 155–56
in New Jersey, 8, 30, 35, 88–90
in New York City, 28–31, 33,
35–36, 49, 86–90, 145–46,
213
in *The New York Times,* 203–4
O'Neill and, 58
Palermo in, 43–44, 47, 69,
71–72
in Philadelphia, 5–8, 32–33,
203–4
pornography and, 48–50
Previte in, 8
Ralph discussing, 9, 14–16,
54–55, 82, 103–4, 125,
130–31, 138, 140, 142, 148,

176, 191–93, 203, 216–17, 235,
238
Rastelli in, 124
Reginelli in, 26
retirement in, 34
Rickshaw Inn for, 79, 81–84
Salerno in, 81, 88–90
Scarfo, N., in, 8, 114–15,
129–30, 168–69
Sindone in, 93
Stanfa, John in, 91–93
Testa, P., in, 17, 114–15
Testa, S., in, 114
Tieri in, 104–6, 125, 127–28
Torano's Italian Bar and
Restaurant for, 110–12
Triangle Civic Improvement
Association for, 104–5
Turchi in, 77, 81
Verna in, 116–17
Virgilio in, 115, 136
Waldorf Astoria Hotel for,
29–30, 35
in *The Wall Street Journal,* 167
Wallace in, 14–15
Weisberg in, 62–64
Young Turks as, 23
mafia ascension
for Bruno, A., 32–41
for Gigante, 104–5
for Gotti, 178–79
for Ralph, 19–25, 52–55, 68,
189–90, 196–205
for Scarfo, N., 116, 149–51
for Stanfa, John, 200–204
for Testa, S., 167–71
mafia ceremony. *See* induction
Manhattan. *See* New York City
Manna, Bobby, 115–16, 136,
149–50, 171
Manni, Jack, 188
Mantle, Mickey, 19–20
Marinucci, Rocco
as hit man, 147–48

Marinucci (*continued*)
  in mafia, 144–45
  murder of, 172–73
marriage, 19, 117–18, 158–59,
  161–62, 215
Marrone, Mike, 77, 81
Martell, Marty, 26
Martorano, George, 153–54
Martorano, Raymond
  ("Long John"), 121
  betrayal by, 150–54
  FBI against, 118
  as hit man, 140
  in mafia, 49, 91, 117–19, 123–24
  murder of, 227
Mathes, James, 225
McCullough, John
  betrayal against, 136–40
  as decoy, 147–48
  murder of, 140
McDevitt (priest), 231–32
McDonnel, Franny, 2–3, 77
McGreal, Joe, xii
  Gotti and, 69–70
  for Local 170, 70
  murder of, 1–3, 7, 74–76
  in prison, 69–71
  for unions, 62, 65–67
Merlino, Joseph ("Skinny Joey"),
  xii, 115, 181, 200
  betrayal against, 225–27, 237–38
  at Bruno wake, 122
  Congress and, 165–66
  for La Cosa Nostra, 219–21
  induction for, 212
  murder attempt on, 202
  prison for, 185–92, 236–38
  Ralph and, 188, 190–97, 203,
    209, 210, 222–23, 225–28,
    236–38
Merlino, Maria, 144, 174
Merlino, Salvatore ("Chuckie"),
  174
  at Bruno wake, 122

as hit man, 168–69
in mafia, 114–15, 144, 176
prison for, 187
Milan, Milton, 223–25
Milicia, Anthony
  ("Tony Machines"), 216
Miller, Ed, 55–56
mob. *See* mafia
Monte, Frank, 129–30
Mr. Living Room, 94–96
murder. *See also* hit men
  of Anastasia, A., 33
  of Avena, 32
  of Barry, 25–27
  of Bianculli, 173
  of Bocchino, 198
  of Bouras, 151–54
  of Bruno, A., 110–14
  of Caponigro, 125–28
  of Castellano, 178
  of Ciancaglini, M., 202–3
  of Cifelli, 168–69
  of DeLuca, 196–97
  of DiAddorio, 198–99
  of DiBernardo, 50
  of Freeney, 66–67
  of Marinucci, 172–73
  of Martorano, R., 227
  of McCullough, 140
  of McGreal, 1–3, 7, 74–76
  of Narducci, F., 171–72
  of Peetros, 151–52
  Ralph discussing, 24
  of Salerno, 126–28
  of Siegel, 43
  of Simone, 128–29
  of Sindone, 129–31
  of Sodano, 213–14
  of Testa, P., 147–48
  of Testa, S., 175–77
  of Tropea, 39–40
  of Turchi, 212
  of Turra, 219
  of Veasey, W., 213

Murder Inc., 61–63
Murray, Jim, 43
Mustache Petes, 23

Narducci, Frank ("Chickie")
   betrayal by, 145–49
   in mafia, 141–42
   murder of, 171–72
Narducci, Frank, Jr., 143
Natale, Carmen, 123, 161–62
Natale, Frankie, 117–18, 120–21
Natale, Grace, 12
Natale, Josephine Ianelli, 11–12
Natale, Lucia, 6, 18–19, 221–22
   FBI and, 98
   mafia and, 120–24, 218–19
   as wife, of Ralph, 117–18,
      158–59, 161–62, 215
Natale, Michael. See Natale,
   "Spike"
Natale, Michael (Ralph son),
   117–18, 120–21
Natale, Michael, Jr., 12, 156–57
Natale, Ralph. See specific topics
Natale, Ralph (grandfather), 11–12
Natale, Rebecca, 161–62
Natale, Sammy, 12
Natale, "Spike," 12–15, 20–22,
   155–56
New Jersey. See also Atlantic City
   Billy Duke's in, 66
   Byrne for, 88
   Garden State Race Track in, 72,
      76, 208, 214, 218
   mafia in, 8, 30, 35, 88–90
   Ralph in, 1, 57, 223–24
   unions in, 57
New York City
   Castellano for, 135–36
   Ferrara Bakery and Café in,
      51–52
   Gotti for, 30, 50, 199–200
   mafia in, 28–31, 33, 35–36, 49,
      86–90, 145–46, 213

   Ralph discussing, 49–50
   Triangle Civic Improvement
      Association in, 104–5
   Waldorf Astoria Hotel in,
      29–30, 35
The New York Times
   mafia in, 203–4
   unions in, 137
Newark. See New Jersey

O'Neill, Tip, 58

Palermo, Frank ("Blinky"), xii
   betrayal against, 107
   in boxing, 43–44, 47
   death of, 214–15
   in mafia, 43–44, 47, 69, 71–72
   prison for, 44
   Ralph and, 208–9
Palm Springs, 57–58
Panisi, Joe, 26–27
Patriarca, Raymond, Jr., 199
Patterson, Floyd, 42
peep shows. See pornography
Peetros, Harry, 151–52
Philadelphia, 20–21
   Budweiser Bar in, 15
   The Friendly Tavern in, 22–23,
      26, 36–38
   Half-Hour Club in, 65
   Italian Market in, 17, 39–40
   Latin Casino in, 61
   mafia in, 5–8, 32–33, 203–4
   the Saloon in, 143–44
   Schmidt's Brewery in, 60, 71
   unions in, 59–60
   Yahn & McCormick in, 17
The Philadelphia Daily News, 223
physical appearance, of Ralph,
   24–25, 55
Pistone, Joe, 204
pornography
   Bruno, A., and, 48–49
   Gambino, C., and, 48–50

pornography (*continued*)
  mafia and, 48–50
  Ralph and, 50
  Show World Center for, 48
Previte, Ron, 8, 209
  for FBI, 216, 218–20, 226
prison
  for Carbo, 44
  Gotti in, 69–70
  for Gravano, 229–30
  Hoffa in, 80
  for Leonetti, 229–30
  Liston in, 42
  for Manna, 115
  McGreal in, 69–71
  for Merlino, J., 185–92, 236–38
  for Merlino, S., 187
  for Natale, "Spike," 13
  for Palermo, 44
  for Ralph, 5–6, 8–9, 96, 99–102,
    116–19, 155–58, 155–60,
    183–85, 207, 219–22, 229–33
  for Scarfo, N., 115, 179–80
  Stanfa, John in, 207
Provenzano, Anthony, 58, 84
Pungitore, Anthony ("Blonde
    Babe"), 143
Pungitore, Joe, 144, 172, 175–76

Ralph. *See* Natale, Ralph
Rastelli, Philip ("Rusty"), 124
rats. *See* betrayal
Reginelli, Marco
  death of, 32–33, 35
  in mafia, 26
religion, 157–58, 231–32
reputation, of Ralph, 24
retirement, in mafia, 34
Riccobene, Harry ("the
    Hunchback"), 23–24
Rickshaw Inn, 79, 81–84
Rifkin, Sam, 61–63
Roth, William, 162–64
Rudman, Warren, 162–64

Ruggiero, Benjamin
    ("Lefty Guns"), 204

Sabella, ("Don Turridu"), 38
Salerno, Tony
  as driver, 104, 106, 108, 112–13
  in mafia, 81, 88–90
  murder of, 126–28
the Saloon, 143–44
Scafidi, Tommy ("Horsehead"), 194
Scarfo, Nicky, xi, 142–43, 145
  betrayal against, 147
  betrayal by, 116, 133–40
  at Bruno wake, 122
  Congress and, 161, 165
  for La Cosa Nostra, 150–51, 171,
    178–79, 187
  as hit man, 133–34
  in mafia, 8, 114–15, 129–30,
    168–69
  mafia ascension for, 116, 149–51
  prison for, 115, 179–80
  Ralph and, 104, 123–24, 134–35,
    150, 164–65, 171, 174–75, 186,
    198
Scarfo, Nicky, Jr.
  at Bruno wake, 122
  murder attempt on, 186–87
Schmidt's Brewery, 60, 71
school, 16–17
Seccio, Ruthann, 215
Show World Center, 48
Sicily, 23, 29–30, 135. *See also*
    La Cosa Nostra
Siedman, Joe, 61–63
Siegel, Benjamin ("Bugsy"), 43
Simone, John ("Johnny Keys"),
    128–29
Sindone, Frank, 104
  betrayal by, 102, 108–9, 110–13
  in mafia, 93
  murder of, 129–31
  Torano's Italian Bar and
    Restaurant for, 110–12

Sodano, Joseph
  murder of, 213–14
South Philly. *See* Philadelphia
Stanfa, Joe, 203
Stanfa, John, xii, 178
  betrayal against, 203–4
  betrayal by, 102, 108–9, 111–14,
    131–32, 179–82
  Bruno, A., and, 92–93, 108–9
  as driver, 111–14
  FBI against, 131–32
  for Gambino, C., 92
  in mafia, 91–93
  mafia ascension for, 200–204
  in prison, 207
  Ralph and, 197–200
  Testa, P., and, 93

teamsters. *See* unions
Testa, Phil ("Chicken Man"), xi
  betrayal against, 116, 146–48
  for Bruno, A., 39–41, 77–78, 111
  at Bruno wake, 122
  for La Cosa Nostra, 129–30, 133,
    135–40, 141–43
  as hit man, 39–40
  in mafia, 17, 114–15
  murder of, 147–48
  Ralph and, 111, 123–24
  Stanfa, John and, 93
Testa, Salvie, xii
  at Bruno wake, 122
  for La Cosa Nostra, 175
  as hit man, 168–69, 171–74
  induction for, 143–44
  in mafia, 114
  mafia ascension for, 167–71
  murder of, 175–77
  Ralph discussing, 167–68, 170,
    172
Tieri, Frank ("Funzi"), 104–6, 125,
  127–28
Torano's Italian Bar and Restaurant, 110–12

Triangle Civic Improvement
  Association, 104–5
Tropea, Pauly, 39–40
Turchi, Ronnie, xii
  betrayal by, 196–97
  in mafia, 77, 81
  murder of, 212
  Ralph and, 210–11
Turra, Anthony, 219

unions. *See also* Local 170
  Baldino for, 62
  for Cadillac Linen Co., 61
  for casinos, 8, 134, 136, 139, 145,
    195
  for La Cosa Nostra, 71
  Daidone for, 225
  Fitzsimmons for, 80–81, 83
  Freeney for, 65–67
  Gerace for, 134, 136–39
  Greeley for, 81–82
  Hanley for, 5–6, 58, 139, 206–7
  Hoffa for, 6–7, 58–61, 80–85
  International Brotherhood of
    Teamsters for, 80
  Local 54, 134, 136, 139, 145, 195
  McGreal for, 62, 65–67
  Miller for, 55–56
  in New Jersey, 57
  in *The New York Times,* 137
  in Philadelphia, 59–60
  Provenzano for, 58, 84
  Ralph and, 6–7, 52–53, 55–60,
    56–60, 62–64, 195, 206–7
  Valli for, 55–56

Vadino, Frankie, xii, 44, 62–63,
  72–73
Valli, Phil, 55–56
Veasey, John, 213
Veasey, William, 213
Verna, Frankie, 116–17
Virgilio, Nicky ("the Blade"), 115,
  136

Waldorf Astoria Hotel, 29–30, 35

The Wall Street Journal, 167

Wallace, George, 14–15

Washington. *See* Congress, US

Weisberg, Willie, 62–64

Williams, Ike, 43

Yahn & McCormick (store), 17

Young Turks, 23

Zeitz, Glenn, 162